Mrs Barbour's Daughters
by AJ Taudevin

Mrs Barbour's Daughters was first produced in 2015
at Oran Mor as part of A Play, A Pie and a Pint in association
with the Traverse Theatre. Mary was played by Anna Hepburn,
Grace by Gail Watson and Libby McArthur played Joan and
Mrs Barbour. The production was directed by Emma Callander,
assisted by Andy McNamee, and featured Sirens of Titan,
Govan Allsorts, Eurydice, Voice Beat, Love Music, Portobello
and Wildfire Women's Community Choirs.

The play was extended and performed at the Tron Theatre
in November 2015 as part of the city-wide centenary
celebrations of the Glasgow Rent Strikes.
Supported by Creative Scotland.

ALBA | CHRUTHACHAIL

CAST

Mary	Anna Hepburn
Grace	Angela Darcy
Joan/Mrs Barbour	Libby McArthur
Choirs	Sirens of Titan, Govan Allsorts, Eurydice, Voice Beat

CREATIVE TEAM

Writer	AJ Taudevin
Director	Andy McNamee
Producer	Dani Rae
Choir Director	Dave Anderson

PRODUCTION TEAM

Production Manager	Dave Shea
Stage Manager	Laura Walshe
Deputy Stage Manager	Fran Craig
Sound/AV Technician	Barry McCall
Lighting Designer	Dave Shea

Produced by Dani Rae in association with the Tron Theatre with thanks to The Traverse Theatre, Michael John O'Neill and the Creative Scotland Producer Project.

BIOGRAPHIES

Dave Anderson is a musician/writer/actor active in theatre since he began with 7:84 in the early 70s. He co-founded Wildcat and wrote/performed with them through the 70s/80s. More recently, he's been producing mini-musicals for A Play, a Pie and a Pint at the Óran Mór. His show *Tir na nOg* was awarded Best New Musical at the Edinburgh Festival in 2007.

Angela Darcy's recent theatre credits include: Janis Joplin: *Full Tilt* (NTS/Regular Music); *The Venetian Twins* (Royal Lyceum); *Whingeing Women* (King's Glasgow); *City of the Blind* (David Leddy/Fire Exit); *Scarfed For Life* (Citizen's Theatre); Goldilocks (Platform); *The 27 Club* (BB Promotions/Forever 27 Productions); *Mister Merlin* (Tron Theatre); *Autobahn* (Theatre Jezebel); *The Tin Forest, Mary Queen of Scots Got Her Head Chopped Off, Our Teacher's A Troll* (National Theatre Of Scotland); *Sub Rosa* (Fire Exit/Citizens' Theatre); *Cinderella* (Byre Theatre/Random Accomplice); *Slick* (Vox Motus); *Shopping For Shoes* (Visible Fictions); *A Very Cosy* Christmas (Tron Theatre) and *The Incredible Swimming Choir* (Starcatchers). Film and Television credits include *High Times, Monarch Of The Glen* and *Rab C* Nesbitt. Angela is also in demand as a voice over artist and has performed in numerous Radio Dramas. As a session singer she performs with many bands all over the UK, she is also a singer/songwriter and the lead singer of Glasgow based Americana/Country band 'The Glass Roots'.

Anna Hepburn has appeared in most theatres throughout Scotland including Dundee Rep, Perth Rep, the Lyceum, Citizens Theatre and Oran Mor. Her one woman play *Consider the Lilies* won a Fringe First at the Edinburgh Festival and went on to tour Scotland, Ireland and Canada. She has also toured with Stellar Quines and Splinters Productions. TV includes *Monarch of the Glen, Rebus, Taggart, Still Game, Young James Herriot* and *River City*. She recently played the role of Granny in *Wooly and Tig* and has appeared in *Dear Frankie*. Anna also writes; two of her plays *Lives o' Men* and *The Penny Pencil* have reached the finals of Community Drama Competitions. Her one woman play *Mary Queen of Scots: The Last Letter* has recently toured Scotland and Canada. Last year she compiled a play commemorating WW1 for her home town of Aberfeldy She can be seen on CBBies at the moment playing Mrs Baxter in *Katie Morag*.

Libby McArthur's work as an actor, writer and director has spanned more than three decades. She has appeared in most of Scotland's returning series, during which she has played wife to Ford Kiernan and Andy Cameron, daughter to Miriam Margoyles, Annie Ross and Johnny Beattie, and sister to Andy Gray, Forbes Masson, and Bobby Carlyle. A popular Daily Record columnist, Libby will be touring in the international comedy success *Mum's The Word* in 2016.

Andy McNamee is a director specialising in new work. He is currently the Senior Reader for the Traverse Theatre and a reader for Playwrights Studio Scotland. He was previously the Trainee Director and Engagement Artist at the Traverse. As director his work includes: *Broth* by Tim Primrose (A Play, A Pie & A Pint & Traverse); *Bear* by Andy McNamee (Old Red Lion) and *Joseph K* by Tom Basden (Linbury Studio.) He has worked as an Assistant Director at the Traverse, The Royal Court and The Pleasance (London.) He trained at The National Theatre Studio and LAMDA.

Dani Rae is a freelance producer, dramaturg and consultant. She has worked with and for some of the UK's leading arts agencies, artists and theatre companies including: Edinburgh Festival Fringe Society, Imaginate, Starcatchers, Gill Robertson, Wee Stories Theatre, Reeling & Writhing, Royal Lyceum, Errol White Company, Plutôt la Vie, Scottish Opera, AJ Taudevin and Magnetic North. Internationally, Dani has worked in Berlin with Chamaeleon Productions and Y2D Productions as booker and PR for their multi award-winning production LEO. She also produces for Wolfgang Hoffmann's Aurora Nova, managing the worldwide rights to Nassim Soleimanpour's *White Rabbit Red Rabbit*, and is Artistic Producer for the Tron Theatre in Glasgow as part of Creative Scotland's Producers' Project.
www.danirae.co.uk

AJ Taudevin's plays include *Some Other Mother*, nominated for the James Tait Black Award 2014, *Chalk Farm*, co-written with Kieran Hurley, which began as a Play, Pie and a Pint and continued to tour internationally as a ThickSkin production, *The 12:57* for Theatre Uncut, *The YelloWing* for the Scottish Mental Health Arts and Film Festival and is a performer and writer in the DM Collective who have created the Óran Mór political variety shows *The Jeans Jacques Rousseau Show, Demons, The Deficit Show* and *To Hell And Back*. She was artist in residence at the Tron Theatre in 2013, one of the Traverse Fifty and she won the Playwrights Studio New Playwrights Award in 2010. As actor Julia Taudevin she has worked for theatre companies including the National Theatre, the National Theatre of Scotland, Catherine Wheels and Magnetic North and her film and TV credits include *Sunshine On Leith* and *Katie Morag*. As a theatre maker she co-directed Kieran Hurley's award-winning plays *Beats* and *Hitch*.

ABOUT THE TRON THEATRE

The Tron is one of Scotland's leading mid-scale producing and presenting theatres, set in the heart of Glasgow's Merchant City.

Housing three performance spaces, rehearsal space, offices, a dedicated Tron Participation workshop space and Tron Bar + Kitchen, the building is a vibrant creative hub, that bustles with activity year-round. The building is also home to Tron Theatre Company, which stages its own productions as well as presenting co-productions and collaborations with other leading theatre companies, alongside a busy programme of high calibre visiting company work.

Dedicated to
David MacLennan.

With thanks to
Mary Lockhart, Catriona Burness, Maria Fyfe, Kieran Hurley,
Henry Bell, Drew Wright and Emma Callander.

Foreword

Mary Barbour's Army Marches On

When I was ten, I recognised that my granny was likely to be a useful historical resource. At school, we had been asked to choose any person from history who was a hero, and to do a project about them. We were to research our hero in any way we liked. I chose Winston Churchill, and went to interview my granny about him.

'Granny, did you know Winston Churchill?' I asked. She was washing her hands of flour, because she had been baking. She turned from the sink,

'Mercy, what makes you ask that?'

'I am doing a project for school on my hero, and it's him'

'Winston Churchill?' said my gentle granny, 'That wicked man wanted to shoot yer Grampa!'

And that was how I began to hear about Red Clydeside. About John MacLean, and Davie Kirkwood, and John Wheatley, and Willie Gallacher, and Jimmy Maxton, and Mannie Shinwell. And about how Winston Churchill has sent the Army into George Square in Glasgow ready to shoot the engineering workers, and in 1921 into Cowdenbeath, to shoot the miners, including my grampa, who had fought in the First World War, and was a hero of the Working Class.

They say the prophet is without honour in his own country. To me, it was not possible that my grandfather, or anybody from Kelty, Cowdenbeath or Ballingry could be a hero. So I began to probe about these Glasgow names. But again, they hardly seemed to me like heroes. They had stood outside on a big Square, and shouted at people about what was wrong with their lives. Then the police had arrested them and put them in prison. And then they had died. But nothing had changed.

'But were there no ladies, Granny? And did none of them make any difference?'

Her face softened. 'Well, there were a few. And they have been forgotten. But the best of them all was called Mrs Barbour. Her name was Mary, like you, and like me, and she led the Rent Strikes, and brought the men out on strike to support the women. And she did make a difference. She got the law changed.'

I am sorry to confess, I remember little of what Granny told me of Mary Barbour beyond that. Again, she did not seem to me to have the glamour, the acts of derring do, the place in history, of Winston Churchill. So, although I did include in my project the fact that Churchill had wanted to shoot my grampa, he remained my hero. But – I was intrigued by, and did not forget, Mrs Mary Barbour.

In the 1980's I lived and worked in Glasgow, and my friend, the late Edna Robertson of the *Glasgow Herald* was one of the few people I encountered who had heard of Mary Barbour. She gave me some photocopies of articles from the *Herald's* archives, including some of a rather stern looking matron in the robes and chain of office of a Baillie. She told me that Mrs Barbour had lived well into the 1950's, and that many people in Govan still remembered her, and held her in high regard.

I spoke to several people in Govan about Mary Barbour, and there was not one who did not smile at her memory. But at that time, Dr Catriona Burness had not started the research hare running, and nobody could point me in the direction of any record of her speeches, or books about her. So in the end, I built own, very personalised picture of the Red Clydesider who is only now beginning to be remembered and celebrated, and who was the inspiration for AJ Taudevin's *Mrs Barbour's Daughters*, for the Remember Mary Barbour campaign for a statue, and for the current political campaign group, Mrs Barbour's Army, of which I am proud to be a founder member.

I can almost see my version Mary Barbour as a living being. I see her, marching full of purpose through Govan. Dancing with children, greeting her women friends, being nodded to by shipyard workers and greeted by name by shop stewards. I feel her energy, her tenacity, her no nonsense, roll up your sleeves and get on with it pragmatism. Her humour and loving kindness. Her working class respectability. Her intelligence and vision. Her sometimes thwarted and disappointed idealism.

Sometimes I am not sure whether I have read of her saying something, or whether I have imagined her saying it. Did she, or did she not say something like, 'If the need is there, the money can, and must be found to meet it?" (I think my friend, the late councillor Agnes Maclean, herself an extraordinary woman who should be remembered for more than her dancing in Cuba, told me she had said that, when I lobbied her support for a funding application for Maryhill Mobile Creche. The voice I hear is still that of Agnes, who was born in Ibrox, and met John MacLean as a child as well as Mary Barbour in her youth, and became a Crane Driver and Rolls Royce Shop Steward.)

I know children loved her. On the first day I marched with Mrs Barbour's Army against the Bedroom Tax, as I was unfurling the banner bearing her name and portrait, three elderly gentlemen watched, and offered help. Then, very shyly, they asked if I would take a picture of them holding the banner. They were old soldiers, wearing RHF regimental ties, and I was puzzled as to why they were so enthusiastic, and why they stood so proudly to attention. I asked – and again saw faces smiling at a fond memory.

> 'She was a great lady. One in a million. Anybody in Govan would tell you that. When we were boys, we would never have seen the seaside if it hadn't been for her. She took us on holiday'

Why are her speeches not recorded, beyond the fact that she did make them? I think it is because she was not an orator. Not a rhetoritician. MacLean, Wheatley. Shinwell, Gallacher and the men of Red Clydeside wanted to move masses of organised workers towards revolution. There's was a resounding rhetoric to put fire in the belly, full of what today we would call soundbites.

Mary Barbour wanted to persuade people. She wanted to empower and give them the confidence to make practical changes in her and their community. She was one of them, and she spoke like one of them, with common sense and shared experience. And she spoke and acted to great effect.

She wanted to make it impossible to increase rents to levels people could not afford. She got the law changed. She wanted women to have secure tenancies. She was a founding member of the Glasgow Women's Housing Association. She wanted women to have control of the number of children to whom they gave birth. She started Family Planning Clincs – and persuaded men to go as well as their wives. She wanted working class people to have means to save and to borrow without profit. She started People's Banks. She wanted an end to the filth and disease, and the dampness caused by attempting to wash and dry bedding in poorly ventilated tenements. She got the council to build wash houses and steamies.

I don't think Mary Barbour went to jail for her beliefs. I think she would have thought that was fine for people with no responsibilities - no close to clean, no man and no children to feed, no friends and neighbours to support. But I think she changed more minds, and had more long term influence, and brought about more immediate change, than all the well documented, well –remembered, well celebrated Red Clydesiders put together.

And she would never have wanted to shoot my grampa.

I am a journalist, a lifelong socialist, co-operator, political and community activist and campaigner. I was Chair of the Scottish Co-operative Party when, inspired by Mary Barbour, and dismayed by the imminent enactment of the Welfare Reform Bill 2012, I founded the campaign and support group, Mrs Barbour's Army. Its distinctive black and white banner has appeared on demonstrations from Glasgow to Perth, Manchester to London, always well supported, and always raising smiles as the women,

men and children who follow it do as Mrs Barbour's campaigners did: bang on pot lids with wooden spoons, and rattle their ricky ticketties – otherwise known as football rattles. The latter day Mrs Barbour's Army also sings songs as it marches … *Bandiera Rosa*, *Bella Ciao*, and *We Shall Overcome* are amongst the favourites.

In addition to marching and demonstrating, members of Mrs Barbour's Army have provided practical support and advice to people in their communities. They were particularly active in the months before the Scottish Government the agreed to mitigate the impact of the Bedroom Tax, and as thousands were in fear of eviction or forced relocation. Members of Mrs Barbour's Army went with other campaigners to stand by people and accompany them to Law Centres or meetings with Landlords, or obstruct those who tried to turn them out of their homes. Several members went to stay with people under such threat, and became lifelong friends.

Mrs Barbour's Army worked with the STUC to organise a coalition of third sector organisations and Scottish civic society to persuade Councils and the Scottish Government to work together on mitigating the Bedroom Tax, and its members chaired and spoke at many meetings and Party Conferences, until eventually the Scottish Government agreed.

During this time, I was working on a zero hours contract as a Care Worker, and was also a family Carer. I saw many resonances in what was happening in the second decade of the 21st Century and what had been happening in the second decade of the 20th. In the 1980's, I had been Co-ordinator of Ruchill Unemployed Workers' Centre, before becoming Community Events Organiser for Mayfest. I remembered large scale plays and musicals which had involved and engaged, and brought activism and hope to communities. Communities, just who were, just as today, oppressed by poverty, cuts, and a government set on the eradication of socialism by the smashing of the working class.

I approached Dave Anderson, with a view to developing an integrated, processed performance and community engagement piece, culminating in a musical production either at Tramway, or outdoors, at Glasgow Green. This piece was to integrate past with present, to draw parallels and explore a continuum. Dave was interested, and they agreed to meet. A couple of weeks later, he had another approach, this time from Maria Fyfe who was keen to have a play about Mary Barbour as part of Oran Mor's A Play, A Pie and a Pint series, to raise awareness and boost the Remember Mary Barbour's Campaign for a statue.

Mrs Barbour's Daughters was the result – an excellent and substantial first step towards the larger project which I still hope to see realised.

Mrs Barbour's Army, meanwhile, goes from strength to strength, campaigning most recently on housing, education and peace, and at the time of writing organising, with a team of volunteers and the Fife People's Assembly, a march and demonstration against Poverty and Cuts in Scotland's Ancient capital, Dunfermline.

Mary Lockhart

MRS BARBOUR'S DAUGHTERS

AJ Taudevin

MRS BARBOUR'S DAUGHTERS

OBERON BOOKS
LONDON

WWW.OBERONBOOKS.COM

First published in 2015 by Oberon Books Ltd
521 Caledonian Road, London N7 9RH
Tel: +44 (0) 20 7607 3637 / Fax: +44 (0) 20 7607 3629
e-mail: info@oberonbooks.com
www.oberonbooks.com

A catalogue record for this book is available from the British
Library.

PB ISBN: 9781783199846
E ISBN: 9781783199853

Cover image by Rachel Campbell

Visit www.oberonbooks.com to read more about all our books
and to buy them. You will also find features, author interviews and
news of any author events, and you can sign up for e-newsletters
so that you're always first to hear about our new releases.

Characters

MARY
Born 1927. 87 and almost totally blind in the present day.

GRACE
Born 1914. Died 2004.

JOAN
Born 1958. 57 in the present day.

MRS BARBOUR
Born 1875, died 1958. Radical activist,
labour activist, women's rights activist,
politician and public speaker.
Appears in this play in 1915
during the Glasgow Rent Strikes.

A note on the play.
The play is set in 2015 and in memories
dating back to 1930.

There should be a choir involved
in the production with members of the choir
sat in the audience throughout.

SCENE ONE
2015

A living room in a tenement flat in Govan. The curtains are drawn even though it is daytime. In the centre of the room is a large arm chair. Beside the chair is a battered saucepan and wooden spoon. Upstage of the chair are two doors – one to the kitchen, the other to the close and the outside world. Between them is a radio. It blares out hits from the 50s and 60s. MARY sits in the armchair, listening to the music, occasionally singing along, perhaps she dances a little in her chair, perhaps she mutters to herself about the singer or the song. She sits like this for some time, content. The song fades.

RADIO: I hope you're all sitting comfortably as we here at Memory Lane Radio wander hand in hand with you back through time. We'll be hearing the news in just a moment …

MARY feels for her pot and spoon, grabs them, at the ready.

RADIO: … but before that, just sit back and relax with this classic hit, recorded in 1968 by the doll faced and honey voiced, blonde bombshell, Tammy Wynette.

Stand By Your Man *starts playing on the radio and MARY relaxes, putting her spoon and pan down. Down at the bottom of the close, JOAN enters the close door and begins making her way up the stairs to MARY's front door. She sings at the top of her voice as she climbs the stairs.*

JOAN: *(Singing.)* I sing of a river I'm happy beside
The song that I sing is the song of the Clyde

MARY: *(Relieved, as JOAN sings.)* There she is.

JOAN: *(Singing.)* Of all Scottish rivers it's dearest to me
It flows from Leadhills all the way to the sea

MARY: *(Fondly, as JOAN sings.)* She's surely got a mind for the words, that woman.

JOAN: *(Singing.)* Oh the River Clyde

MARY: *(Singing along, mischievously.)* The pong of the Clyde.

JOAN: *(Singing.)* The Wonderful Clyde
The name of it thrills me and fills me with…

JOAN is at MARY's front door. Short of breath, she enters the flat and dumps her coat and bag.

JOAN: Wooft. I'll be glad when I don't have to hike up those stairs again.

MARY: Whisht.

JOAN drops a bag of shopping into the kitchen, fishes out her mobile phone to check if there have been any calls. There haven't. She resolves to remain positive.

JOAN: *(Singing.)* And I'm satisfied
Whate'er may betide

MARY: Hush your whisht.

JOAN: The sweetest of songs is the song of the Clyde
Doo diddle doo doo diddle doo doo diddle diddle diddle diddle doo…

MARY: I cannae hear the radio with all that diddledooing.

JOAN: Come on Mary, give us a wee diddle doo of your own.

MARY: Diddle doo yourself out of here.

JOAN: I'm only just in the door. You're not wanting to see the back of me already are you?

MARY: I'd love to see anything at all.

JOAN: Aye, well, you've still got your voice, eh? Come on, sing with me.
(Singing.) Stand by your man

MARY: Oh you!

JOAN: Come on Mary!
(Singing.) Send out for pudding suppers
When you're up on your uppers

(Speaking.) Come on, Mary, you know the words!

(Singing.) Oh is it any wonder

(Speaking.) How does it go?

MARY: *(Singing.)* You cannae stand the skunner

JOAN: That's it!

They sing together

MARY/JOAN: Stand by your man!

They laugh. The radio continues, it should play as a quiet, barely intelligible burble underneath the dialogue.

RADIO: Yes that was *Stand by Your Man* originally released in 1968 where it reached number one in the US country charts for three weeks rocketing Wynette from vaguely successful country singer to superstar almost overnight. It reached number one in the UK Singles Chart in 1975 and is one of the most covered songs in the history of country music. Well, speaking about standing by your man, let's wander further back in time together to the early 1940s where I've got a real treat for the ladies. Well, and the gentlemen too, those of you who can remember the 1940s, I don't know about you but my Mrs is my mobile brain, aren't you Mags? Mags the mobile brain. Ho ho.

MARY: You're a wicked woman.

JOAN: Two voices are always stronger than one.

MARY: Aye, but even one voice can be trouble enough.

JOAN: We're a family of voices. My mother always said that.

MARY: Grace? Ha! Grace never shut up.

JOAN: She's said hee haw for ten year now.

MARY: And I've had you whittering away ever since.

JOAN: Come on now, River City and a cup of tea twice a week wasnae that bad was it?

MARY: It's the last two years you being here every waking minute that does my heid in.

JOAN: Ach, I know you love me really Aunty Mary.

MARY: Do I now?

MARY: Are you wanting to go back to one of your old council carers?

MARY: Lazy, layabout good for nothing muckle clyping galoots!

JOAN: Remember that's my lot you're talking about if that agency would ever give me a call.

MARY: Leaving me in my ain mess for hours on end.

JOAN: I know there's no excuse but everyone is just doing the best they can with what little time they have.

MARY: Council care? Is that not an oxymijiggy? Moron. That's the one. Ha! Council morons. Wouldnae know a hoover if it hit them in the face.

JOAN: Let's open the curtains, shall we?

MARY: Not yet.

JOAN: It's baltic in the close now everybody else has moved out. And you'll notice the difference in the light, I promise you. Sunny Govan is surely earning its name the day. Even managed to pop hame and put a wash on. Had a tiny wee lie doon on my ain bed, watched the sunlight dance aff the Clyde out the windae.

MARY: *(Referring to the radio.)* Oooo! What song has that rascal got for me now?

JOAN: They new goose feather pillaes I got with the vouchers you gave me must be a dream tae sleep a whole night on. I ordered two more for your room and all, so you'll have a soft landing when you flit.

MARY: I flitted here fae your mothers and I'm never flitting again.

JOAN: You'll just sink into the ground along with the rest of the building will you?

MARY: Will you shut your yabbering.

JOAN: Even the Pudleski's have gone, Mary, you are the last Mohican in the close.

MARY: Bah.

JOAN: The bailiff will be here to evict you any day.

MARY: I need tae hear the singing!

JOAN: What'll you have with your tea? I've only got Club Biscuits or Custard Creams.

MARY: You're drowning out my only joy with your hullabaloo.

JOAN: Custard Cream?

MARY: I need tae hear what song it is.

JOAN: Or a Club?

MARY: You'll get a club round the heid in a minute if you're not careful.

JOAN: Club it is.

JOAN exits.

RADIO: That's right, let's head on back to 1942 to be precise when the world was enthralled to a woman of great power, skill and ingenuity. Moving from whipping cake mixes with an electric mixer to operating the drill that would keep our boys' planes in the skies, it's the one, the only, the greatest heroine of the Second World War, Rosie the Riveter.

The song Rosie the Riveter *starts. MARY is delighted. She begins to clap and sing along to the song. The radio fades, we slip into her memory.*

SCENE TWO
1942

MARY is 14 years old. She is singing Rosie the Riveter.

MARY: *(Singing.)* Rosie brrrrrrr the riveter.

GRACE, 27, appears out of the bedroom.

GRACE: Will you shut your geggie, the boys are asleep.

MARY: Gracie! They're taking girls on at the Rolls Royce factory making parts for the planes that'll be flying over your Tommy.

GRACE: You're not old enough for that sort of work.

MARY: I will be next month. Fifteen. That's the age the lady I met on Bath Street said I had to be.

GRACE: Keep your voice down.

MARY: Have you heard what it's like for the girls who work there, Grace? They put on dances for you in the evenings and the American GIs line up to kiss you and birl you round and round till your head goes dizzy and your heart's about to burst.

GRACE: And then you have to ride on the bus hame for hours only to get up a moment later for another shift on the same job a man would get paid double for.

MARY: That's no different from you at Templeton's.

GRACE: Mibbes aye, but if the man comes back fae war to claim his job at Rolls Royce, that'll be you out on your ear.

MARY: That won't matter because by then my hand will be promised in marriage to one of those handsome GIs. He'll whisk me away to Kansas to live on a prairie where we'll have a beautiful baby daughter with perfect golden ringlets and bright blue eyes. And I'll spend the rest of my life making her pretty little dresses and tying ribbons in her hair and watching the wind blow blossom over my handsome husband working in the fields as I sit on the porch eating scones and butter.

GRACE: Do you know why Rolls Royce are taking more women on? Because we are not winning this war. Mark my words, within the next month your handsome young men will be bloody corpses rotting in mountains of the dead.

MARY: Gracie!

GRACE: Life isn't a fairytale, Mary. The likes of us are lucky enough if we get fae one day to the next. Days filled with toil and nights filled with fear. There's only one thing that will change that and it does not involve dancing and hallooing with American soldiers.

MARY: The lady said they need me.

GRACE: Who really needs you, eh? If you want work, there's plenty of pamphlets fae the Women's Welfare and Advisory Clinic I can give you to hand out. There's nae money in it but we'll find you other paid work more fitting for a girl your age.

MARY: I don't want to pamphleteer.

GRACE: How no?

MARY: I just … I don't want to.

GRACE: Are you ashamed of this family?

MARY: No. I'm just not like you.

GRACE: Mammy would want you to. She'd've jumped for joy to see her two lassies getting word out about the ways to avoid having that next bairn without the men knowing about it.

MARY: Gracie…

GRACE: She would! I know she'd've backed Mrs Barbour supporting the clinic even if most other socialists frowned on her when she did.

MARY: What do I care about Mrs Barbour?

GRACE: Shame on you. All of you bairns have her to thank for even being alive.

MARY: I thought that was Mr Churchill?

GRACE: Mr Churchill is a warmongering bawheid who cares nothing for the likes of you and me. Mark my words young Mary, in years to come that man'll be the symbol of all that is rotten about Great Britain.

MARY: Well, I suppose he is ugly.

GRACE: He has the face of a dog licking piss aff a nettle.

MARY: Like this.

MARY makes a face.

GRACE: Worse.

MARY makes an uglier face. They laugh.

GRACE: Ya wee bissom! What's happened, sweetheart? It's not like you to be so hard on Mrs Barbour.

MARY: I don't want to be like her.

GRACE: Who do you want to be like then?

MARY: Joan Fontain, Betty Davis, Ingrid Bergman.

GRACE: God protect us fae lipstick, heels and hair pins.

MARY: How about Rosie?

GRACE: Who?

MARY: Rosie the Riveter! She's all blood, sweat and tears. Well, sweat anyway. And she still looks smashing.
(Singing.) Rosie's got a boyfriend, Charlie
Charlie he's a Marine…

GRACE: You've woken the boys with your hullaballoo. Go and hush them back to sleep.

GRACE: *(Singing.)* Rosie's got a boyfriend, Charlie…

MARY: Ach, no, you'll fill their heads with nonsense. Here, you scrub they dishes clean. All your talk of Rolls Royce has put me in mind of a lullaby I learned fae yet another Mary.

GRACE exits. She sings. MARY sits listening.

GRACE: *(Sings.)* Oh dear me, the mill's gaen fast
The puir wee shifters canna get a rest
Shifting bobbins coarse and fine
They fairly mak you work for your ten and nine
Oh dear me, I wish the day were done
Running up and down the pass is nae fun
Shiftin, piecin, spinnin, warp, weft and twine
To feed and clathe ma bairnies affen ten and nine

MARY'S attention drifts and she begins to hum Rosie the Riveter *quietly over GRACE's singing, but the words of GRACE's final verse can still be clearly heard.*

Oh dear me the warld's ill divided
Them that works the hardest are aye wi least provided
But I maun bide contented dark days or fine
There's nae much pleasure livin affen ten and nine

SCENE THREE
2015

Rosie The Riveter *plays and MARY sings along gently. JOAN enters.*

JOAN: A family of voices so we are.

MARY: You wouldnae know a good tune if you met it in your soup. Brought up on your mother's commie clap trap so you were.

JOAN: Time to let the sunshine in.

MARY: Not yet, Joan.

JOAN: You need your Vitamin D.

MARY: I get all the vitamins I need in my porridge.

JOAN: I've not worked in this field for over thirty years to have you tell me what you need. Now cover over your eyes.

MARY, covers her eyes, JOAN opens the curtains and exits back into the kitchen, tidying as she goes. Light falls onto MARY's face. She clasps her hands onto her eyes to keep out the light. The song on the radio fades out.

RADIO: Wasn't Rosie just riveting?! Yes, see what I did there? Or should I say, hear what I did there? Ho ho. Yes, folks, you're listening to Memory Lane Radio bringing you hits right back through history. It's is 11am and time for the news. David Cameron has announced plans to further slash benefits for pensioners / in a bid to get the economy back on track. Other cuts include a reduction in the value of attendance allowance – those paid to look after relatives – and disability allowances for OAPs.

MARY feels for and grabs her saucepan and wooden spoon and begins to bang loudly to drown out the news. JOAN enters. She turns off the radio.

MARY: Turn that wireless on!

JOAN: I'll turn it on in a minute.

MARY: I need to hear when the singing starts again.

JOAN: Mary, I promise I'll turn it on when the news is finished.

In protest, MARY starts to bang her pot with her spoon.

JOAN: Mary.

MARY: Turn it up!

JOAN: Will you please put the pan and spoon down?

MARY: I need to hear when the singing comes on again.

MARY continues to bang her pot. JOAN tries different tactics.

JOAN: *(Singing.)* Come on, come on and get happy

You've got to chase all your cares away …

MARY bangs her pot louder.

JOAN: *(Singing.)* We're caught in a trap
I can't walk out
Because I love you too much Mary…

MARY bangs even louder.

JOAN: I'll sing The Internationale next if you don't stop that banging.

MARY stops.

JOAN: I can always count on one of my mother's favourites, can't I?

MARY: Your mother might have sung songs about us all being united but who was the one left scrubbing her floors and running after her weans? Eh? There was nothing amazing about Grace.

JOAN checks her phone again.

JOAN: Ach well, looks like they've got nae hours for me today. Just as well, I couldnae get out anyway. They're blocking all the roads aff. Must be a parade or something. All they red traffic hingmies out. You know the ones. Like what they put on that statues heid down on Queen Street. What did they put on his heid before they had they red traffic hingmies that's what I want to know. Maybe just as well…

MARY begins to bang the spoon on the pan again.

JOAN: *(Singing.)* Stand up you victims of oppression…

MARY stops banging.

MARY: A wicked woman. Just like your mother.

JOAN: Aye, well, if that's true, I must be a wee bit like you and all.

MARY: I'm nothing like your mother was.

JOAN: Aye you are. Amazing woman that you are, Mary.

MARY: No decency. No dignity. No decorum.

JOAN: I'll get your tea on.

JOAN exits, humming Amazing Grace.

SCENE FOUR
1953

GRACE, 39, appears in MARY's memory. She is dressed in funeral attire. She hum-sings, distracted at first, but as the scene establishes she becomes increasingly wild, flinging things about in the flat looking for something.

GRACE: … how sweet …

that saved a wretch like me

'Tis Grace that brought … thus far

… will lead me…

MARY: *(Gently.)* Gracie? Can I help?

GRACE: Have you seen my Paisley shawl?

MARY: You're not wearing red. Not today.

GRACE: I need my Paisley shawl.

MARY: Let's just set down quietly with a cup of tea.

GRACE: I can set down quietly when I'm deid.

MARY: Grace. The Lord giveth and the Lord …

GRACE: The only lord in this house gave me that red Paisley shawl the day he married me and now I've gone and lost the damned thing.

MARY: What do you need it for?

GRACE: To go out, ya wally!

MARY: Not today of all days.

GRACE: Says who, Mrs Woman?

MARY: Please don't cry me that.

GRACE: You're a woman.

MARY: I'm no one's missus.

GRACE: How about that Murdo MacLeod? I've seen the way he looks at you.

MARY: Grace, you need to sit down. Just sit down and maybe have a wee listen to the wireless and a nice cup of tea.

MARY puts on the wireless.

RADIO: And now, Queen Elizabeth the Second, having been thus anointed and crowned, shall follow every part of the Benediction with a loud and hearty Amen. The Lord bless you and / keep you The Lord protect you in all your ways. And prosper all your handywork.

GRACE: No. No. No. No. No. Aff with her heid!

GRACE turns the wireless off violently.

MARY: Gracie!

GRACE: No time for the Queen. No time for the wireless. No time for tea. The meeting starts in an hour.

MARY: Naebody will be at the meeting. Half the congregation were your Independent Labour Party and they'll all be down the pub toasting your husband's memory. As you should be doing yourself right now with a nice cup of tea.

GRACE: I'll not be darkening the ILP's door again. There are new doors opening. This very day in fact. The Scottish National Assembly of Women! Of women! Women, Mary, women! Actual, real, working women without whom the entire fabric of our society would crumble. So the Queen can go and bite her royal bahooky.

MARY: Grace, you need to calm down.

GRACE: And Mrs Barbour will be there. Speaking! At 78!
78! Can you imagine what the world must look like from 78?
Where's my Paisley shawl?

MARY: You're staying right here in this house.

GRACE: I stayed five years stuck in this house wishing
Tommy'd come home safe from fighting the Nazis and eight
more wishing he hadn't for all the torment it caused him. Ach,
the shawl can go to hell, I'm away. Will you watch the weans
or will I chap Mrs Bain's door?

MARY: Gracie, your meetings are all well and good but they're
too wee to change a hair on anyone's head.

GRACE: You've clearly never walked through a cloud of
midges.

MARY: Nothing you or I do or say is of any importance to
anyone.

GRACE: Mary, this world is run by men. Royal or wealthy
men, or working men with one fist in the air for liberty and
the other clamped firmly over his wife's or his sister's or his
daughter's mouth.

MARY: I won't let you go. You're not yourself.

GRACE: I'm alive, Mary. You're alive. Alive! Here, hold my
hands. Hold them! Feel that warmth. Feel the life. Your life!
My life! Feel our blood warming our flesh. Feel our blood
pumping through our hearts, our chests, our arms and seeping
out between our legs.

MARY: Grace!

GRACE: Mary! You are a young and strenuous fighter.
Who said that? Go on! Who said that?

MARY: Stop shouting.

GRACE: Who said it?

MARY: I don't know. Mrs Barbour?

GRACE: Do you not remember the story mammy used to tell us about when she took me to see Mrs Barbour stand down fae the ILP? She was some woman wur mammy. Took me on the rent strikes before I could barely walk.

MARY: How could I forget that.

GRACE: So you must remember the ILP story!

MARY: Oh aye. I'm the glaikit wee sister.

GRACE: 'The difficulties ahead,' Mrs Barbour said 'the difficulties ahead require young and strenuous fighters.' I mind mammy squeezing my hand and whispering 'That's you, that is.' And winking her blue eye down at me.

MARY: You and wur mammy.

GRACE: And now you are that young and strenuous fighter, Mary.

MARY: No. That's what you want me to be.

GRACE: You know the words. The songs have been sung to you since you were born.

MARY: Oh I know the songs.

GRACE: Aye you do.

MARY: Aye, I do.

GRACE: Sing for me!

MARY: Gracie…

GRACE: Sing!

MARY: Sing?

GRACE: SING!

Impulsively, mischievously, MARY begins to sing to the tune of the Internationale:

MARY: *(Singing.)* Arise ye women fae depression

You've no need tae be so dour
We know ye'd like tae have possessions
But ye cannae cos you're so damned poor

GRACE: *(Laughing.)* You're a wicked woman so you are!

MARY: *(Singing.)* Nae man who earns a mint will have you
Cos you're stuck wi yer sister's weans
Nae job will give you a promotion
Cos you've got a woman's brain

GRACE: *(Laughing.)* Daftie!

MARY: *(Singing.)* So come all ye dafties
Come and be a communist
Yer sister and her lassies
Do talk a load ay pish

> *GRACE disappears. MARY is pulled back to the present.*

SCENE FIVE
2015

MARY: Gracie? Grace.

> *Pause.*

MARY: *(Singing, gently.)* So comrades come rally
And the last fight let us …
The internationale …

> *She cannot remember the words.*

MARY: Joan. Joan! Joan!

> *JOAN enters.*

JOAN: What is it? What's wrong?

MARY: You need tae turn the wireless on. I'm missing the singing.

> *JOAN turns on the radio*

RADIO: ... for the union has voiced concern over staff at the recently opened Queen Elizabeth University Hospital in Govan/ continuing to have to rent private parking spaces from nearby residents ...

MARY grabs her pan and spoon and begins to bang.

MARY: No! No! No!

JOAN turns off the radio.

JOAN: Will you not just let me change the station?

MARY: No. That's my Memory Lane. Did me fine until you came along and brought my sister with you. Filling up my heid with memories of her.

JOAN: It was your choice to come to her funeral.

MARY: I never had a choice.

JOAN: Never had a choice! Sitting right in the front row next to me. Me who you'd never even met. Scowling at my big brothers like they were the cause of all your misery and greeting intae your hankie like it was your ain mother that had died.

MARY: I was greetin for my mother that day. The only person who ever really cared for me.

JOAN: My mother cared for you.

MARY: The only person your mother cared for was herself. Picketing and posturing and piddling about with her heid in the clouds while everyone around her had to scurry around picking up the pieces that come with living in the real world. She'd demand the very skin aff someone's back if she could. And you? Ha! You just gave in to her demands like she was some kind of queen didn't you?

JOAN: Aye she was demanding. Me, chapping her door in the dead of night, battered and bruised, after months drinking an ocean. She demanded more of me than that. And thank Christ she did.

JOAN checks her phone.

JOAN: Bastards!

Silence.

MARY: I'm sorry for what's happened to you, hen.

JOAN: I'm not.

MARY: I'm sorry they've no got any hours for you.

JOAN: Ach, I'm one of the lucky ones. At least being your designated carer I know I'll never actually have zero hours work in a week.

MARY: I'm glad I'm not a total waste of space then.

JOAN: Mary, I'm going to start packing your things. It's time for you to come down the road with me.

MARY: Is that not the kettle I can hear?

JOAN: It's three weeks since I last had a night in my ain bed.

MARY: That's the kettle boiled.

JOAN: I'm barely making my payments on a house I never get to sleep in.

MARY: I'll have my tea now, ta.

JOAN: How do I know the council isnae going to bring in some new tax charging me a pound of flesh for every night I sleep away fae home?

MARY: Nice cup of tea and a Club Biscuit.

JOAN: A pound of flesh for you and me to sleep in a tenement that's half sunk intae the ground when I've got a two bed new build just down the road.

MARY: A nice Club Biscuit.

JOAN: A two bed new build right on the river, endless sunlight, a kitchen you could swing two cats in, a toilet that flushes on the first go, double glazing, fresh air, and goose feather pillaes…

MARY: I'll get my own tea. Ta ta now, thanks for stopping by.

MARY rises from the chair and almost immediately collapses.

MARY: Joan! Joan!

JOAN catches her and helps her back into the chair.

JOAN: It's alright.

MARY: Oh Joan.

JOAN: You're alright.

MARY: I cannae …

JOAN: There you go.

JOAN: I cannae …

JOAN: Breathe. That's it. That's it. Breathe. There you go. Feeling better now?

MARY: It's just my back. It's a wee bit stiff, that's all.

JOAN: That'll be my line soon, me sleeping on that sofa of yours.

MARY: They want me to go into a home. Sitting all day listening to drool drip fae the mouths of mindless eejits in nappies. They cannae do that to me.

JOAN: You don't have to do what they want you to do. What was it my mother used to say? If the government won't defend our basic rights …

MARY: Wasnae your mother said that.

JOAN: Who was it then?

MARY: Mrs Barbour, that's who.

JOAN: *(Taken aback.)* Mrs Barbour?

MARY: It wasnae Grace. Nothing good ever came out of Grace.

Pause.

JOAN: I'll put the bins out.

JOAN exits to the kitchen.

MARY: Turn that wireless on! Hoy! Joan! The wireless! They'll have stopped yabbering on about all the rubbish now.

JOAN walks through from the kitchen with a bin bag, turns on the wireless and exits through the front door.

RADIO: … there was nothing like it was there? Heading down to the Barras for a night on the tiles. And did you know it was built by a woman? My Mags was at some event celebrating the forgotten women of Glasgow and wrote that down for me. Oh, she knows what'll surprise me does my Mags. A Mrs Margaret McIver built it apparently. So, in memory of that other Mags, here's a hit, recorded in the same year the Barrowland Ballroom was built…

Goodnight My Love *begins to play. MARY sits. Content at first, but soon troubled and transfixed by a memory. The song fades.*

SCENE SIX
1934

MARY is now 7. She sits. Still and silent. Lost. GRACE, 20, enters. She responds to MARY as if MARY has spoken, but we never hear MARY speak.

GRACE: She's gone. There's nothing can be done.

I want her too. But she's gone. And there's nothing can be done about it. You're to come live with me and Tommy and the babby in Fairfield now.

I know you do but sometimes we don't get to choose what happens in life.

Here, how would you like to go to the seaside with wee James? Just the two of you?

That's right. And Mrs Barbour.

Well done! Mrs Mary Barbour. You're fair lucky to be named after such a great woman you know. Given her life to people like us, so she has. See the baths and the wash houses and the play grounds? That's thanks to her. See your wee drink of milk you get at school every day? You can thank her for that and all. Aye, we're lucky to have her. And me and you are the luckiest of all because now she's retired she's taking weans like you and wee James away to the seaside. The seaside Mary! The sea! Can you imagine what the sea looks like?

I suppose it must look like … Well, I suppose it must look like an endless blue Clyde. Don't you think?

Will you go and see it for me and tell me what it's like?

What is it darling?

I don't know if mammy is in heaven.

I hope so too. If it exists.

Here, will I sing you one of wur mammy's favourites songs? Aye? We'll sing it and then we'll pack up your things. Now mind you listen tae the words for when you're alone and wanting to know what mammy might say to you, you can remember the song and the words'll be there tae help you find the way forward.

GRACE sings first as a lullaby to MARY but as the song builds, she moves away from MARY, singing it directly to the audience, a direct and honest delivery.

Come all ye false historians

You hide us from the truth

A story I would tell to you

All starting in my youth

From lovely Lowther's mossy banks

My rivulets begin

And down and through the Lanark glade

And by the Calder's lin

I nurtured all the silven glades

Where cutters tilt their fields

And many's the pleasant summers hence

These crops are bound to yield
On sunlit beams and golden streams
I wandered wild and free
Till I joined the tide at the estuary wide
And I danced into the sea
I saw the Glasgow fishermen
Their little shielins build
I saw the lads deprive them of
The very land they tilled
Likewise the poor guid weavin folk
Who laboured night and day
Their weary sleep so troubled deep
Their lives so hard and grey
Likewise the Lanark miners too
A similar fate endured
In smelters doon by walkin fields
These legions of the poor
And when they rose against their foe
For me twas no surprise
'Neath morn and e'en old Clyde has seen
The anguish in their eyes
Till there arose upon its banks
A stalwart breed of them
They swore that they would never be
poor sufferin slaves again
With all their might and courage stood
Nor did they stand in vain
What joy for me to live to see the likes of John Maclean
Their emblem was the banner red
They were no craven crew
As Clyde has nurtured with its streams
They lived and fought for you

Their names will keep throughout the years
Unchanged by time nor tide
For liberty come sing with me this ballad of the Red Clyde

A moment of silence. GRACE exits, leaving MARY alone. MARY begins to weep. Slowly, slowly the radio returns as she weeps.

SCENE SEVEN
2015

Goodnight My Love *is still playing on the radio. MARY is weeping. JOAN enters with a letter.*

JOAN: Postie didnae even bother coming up the ... Mary?

MARY: They're all dead.

JOAN: Not quite. There's me. And my brothers. And their weans.

MARY: I'm not talking about you.

JOAN: Oh.

MARY: I don't need you. Off you go now.

JOAN: You're not wanting me to read your mail to you?

MARY: Ta ta. Bye bye.

JOAN: How about that cup of tea? The kettle's boiled.

MARY: It boiled fifty year ago.

JOAN: Aye, feels like it. Here. Dry your eyes.

JOAN hands MARY a hankie.

JOAN: Time staunds still for not a one of us.

JOAN exits to the kitchen. The song on the radio ends.

RADIO: Well, they just don't sing em like they used to, isn't that right? Let's leap forward a couple of decades and turn things up a notch with a personal favourite from 1958, the one, the only Perry Como with *Magic Moments.*

MARY: 1958?

> Magic Moments *begins to play.* JOAN *enters with the open letter, turns the radio down.*

MARY: Hoy! Turn that up. That was the year I went out with Murdo MacLeod.

> *Pause.*

MARY: Are you deaf? I said turn that music up.

> JOAN *turns the radio off.*

JOAN: They've set the final date. You've got till Monday before the bailiffs come.

MARY: They've no right.

JOAN: Mary. The foundations are rotten. We're sinking into the ground as we speak.

MARY: They've no right, locking me away in a home.

JOAN: You don't have to go into a home. You can move in with me.

MARY: You don't mean that.

JOAN: I do.

JOAN: It's a terrible idea.

MARY: My brothers think it's a good one.

MARY: Ha! Your brothers think that do they?

JOAN: We all do.

MARY: You're just like her.

JOAN: Don't bring my mother into this. This is about you and me.

MARY: Never cared about a soul but herself.

JOAN: Mary, we don't have time for this.

MARY: Snatching me from the only place I could ever call home. Just like your mother did. An orphan I was. And she swooped in and dragged me off to care for your scabby brothers with their snotty noses and language fae the gutter. While she swanned about thinking herself a queen of the people. Grace the Disgraced. That's what she was!

JOAN: Ach, go to hell.

JOAN grabs her coat and bag.

MARY: Grace the Disgraced, Queen of the gutter!

Impulsively, JOAN adjusts the radio tuner to a news station, turns it up loud and then exits out the front door. MARY shouts over the radio.

RADIO: The chief executive of the Independent Parliamentary Standards Authority said the economy was recovering, politicians were being underpaid and a commitment to the 10% pay increase was a necessary measure to ensure good MP candidates who are accustomed to higher pay are not excluded from Parliament …

MARY: Turn it off! Off! Turn that devil off! Hoy! Joan! Joan! Where are you? Joan? Joan! Come back here! Joan! Joan? Joan? Joan! …

MARY grabs the pot and spoon and begins to bang in rage, closing her eyes and willing the world around her to fade. The radio fades.

SCENE EIGHT
1958

MARY is now 31, sitting in the same armchair and banging her pot with her spoon in rage. GRACE, 44, enters. GRACE takes the saucepan and spoon from Mary.

GRACE: What in God's name is wrong with you? I can hear you half way down the street!

MARY: It's Murdo. He's tae marry Sheila Smeaton.

GRACE: I never trusted that Murdo McLeod.

MARY: He was meant to marry me. No one'll have me now.

GRACE: There's more to life than having a man. You've got your job, and this flat, thanks to Mrs Barbour's campaign for …

MARY: Leave that mad auld boot out of it.

GRACE: We were like daughters to that woman.

MARY: I'm only one woman's daughter.

GRACE: Aye, but you were raised on her words never the less.

MARY: If Mrs Barbour had any words worth listening to I'd hear them on the wireless or read them in the newspaper. She'd be taught in schools and her story written in history books, not the prattlings of mad wifies stuck in their memories of the past!

GRACE: You will rue the day you can no longer remember her words.

MARY: She was your poor house heroine. Not mine. I have no one.

GRACE: You have me.

MARY: I will die alone and lonely and you will be long dead and buried.

GRACE: You'll have the boys.

MARY: Ha!

GRACE: I will make them promise to care for you after I am gone. All of them. The boys and the baby.

Pause.

MARY: The what?

GRACE: The baby.

MARY: You're pregnant?

GRACE: Apparently so.

MARY: A pregnant widow. At forty-four.

GRACE: I did everything I could to prevent it.

MARY: Not everything, clearly.

GRACE: I shouldn't have told you. I should've waited.

MARY: Until what? Until you were married?

GRACE: I'll not marry again. I couldn't do that to Tommy.

MARY: Tommy's been dead five years.

GRACE: It was an accident, Mary. A foolish accident, agreed, but one that's going to give us a great amount to be thankful for. I feel certain it's a girl this time.

MARY: Well bully for you.

GRACE: Haven't you always said you wanted a baby girl?

MARY: A baby girl of my own, Grace. I want a baby girl of my own.

GRACE: And there'll come a day when you will have one but until then you'll have this bundle of joy.

MARY: I am not raising another child of yours.

GRACE: I am not asking you to.

MARY: Oh, no, you never ask.

GRACE: I shouldn't have to ask. It's what sisters do. You help raise my weans just as I will help raise yours.

MARY: I will never have weans.

GRACE: You might if you spent less time flapping about thinking the whole world is against you.

MARY: I spend my days working my fingers to the bone and what do I get at the end of it? I get to run after your boys and keep your house while you're away pushing the word of the devil into every ear that will listen. I'll never have a family like you have.

GRACE: For God's sake you're only thirty-one!

MARY: And I will grow old with dignity, dear sister, unlike your good self. Have you not heard? You'll be laid off after that bairn is born. That's the new law coming in. Templeton's will have tae give you the boot and you'll be learnt your proper place at long last.

GRACE: Never.

MARY: You're a disgrace, Grace. Ha! Grace the Disgraced!

GRACE: *(Singing, defiantly.)* Oh we are women

MARY: Be quiet.

GRACE: *(Singing.)* And we are marching

MARY: Do not start.

GRACE: *(Singing.)* Oh Bella Ciao Bella Ciao Bella Ciao Ciao

MARY: Do not sing that filth in my house.

GRACE: *(Singing.)* Oh we are marching
For liberation
Oh Bella Ciao Ciao Ciao Ciao Ciao!

MARY: Get out. I never want to see you again.

GRACE: You don't mean that.

MARY: I do.

GRACE: You cannae mean it. We're sisters.

MARY: In blood we are. But nothing else.

The memory ends abruptly, MARY is yanked back into the present.

SCENE NINE
2015

The radio is suddenly very loud. MARY is distraught, torn between her memories and the present, unable to find peace. She searches for her spoon and pan but cannot reach it.

RADIO: ... bought the housing estate for £140 million and has hiked rents up by between three and four hundred pounds a month forcing over 90% of the resident families into destitution. When asked to respond to local Labour MP Doreen Miller's comments that the evictions were creating chaos in a previously harmonious community, the Tory MP said it was nothing compared to the chaos in the Labour party which is only serving to strengthen his own party...

The radio crackles and MARY leaps into another memory.

SCENE TEN
1931

The radio is on. MARY is an infant, curled up on her chair, listening.

RADIO: ... Oswold Mosley, formerly of the Conservative Party before crossing the floor to join Ramsay MacDonald's Labour government, has announced the formation of the New Party sparking concern amongst the cabinet and proletariate alike as to what this new form of British fascism will mean for the ...

GRACE, 15, enters in a flurry, turns off the radio and grabs the pan and spoon, handing it to MARY. MARY is active but we never hear her speak.

GRACE: Bang bang bang that pan, wee Mary! We'll see if mammy can hear us down in the street.

GRACE runs to the window, waves.

Ta ta now mammy! Never you worry, me and wee Mary will keep the roof over our heads while you're away tae work. Ta ta!

MARY stops banging.

Now, you and me are to rake out the fire and build it anew, take the ashes doon to the midden, darn the socks, turn the sheets and scrub the close steps. But first … shall we play at fighting the landlord hun?

MARY bangs the pan with enthusiasm.

Right. You can be me and I'll be wur mammy.

'Hush now little Gracie, we've no time for your greeting. Your daddy may be away fighting the hun but we've got wur ain battle tae fight here at hame agin they nasty landlords.'

MARY starts to bang the pot and pan

Not yet! That's for later. First Mrs Barbour has tae call up to us fae the back court. You can be Mammy, and, here, Mammy's shawl can be me and I'll be Mrs Barbour.

I'll stand up here on this like it's the midden out in the back court there.

GRACE grabs the pan and bangs it.

'Women of Govan!'

No you don't say anything back you just listen. You and all the women you're just hanging out the windaes and listening.

'Women of Govan! We have more power than these men in their bowler hats and suits! We have each other!'

You can cheer at that.

'And so I ask you! Will we stand for this injustice?'

You're meant to shout never. Let's shout it together, two voices are aye better than one.

'Will we stand for this injustice?'

NEVER.

Louder!

'Will we stand for this tyranny?'

Bang your pot!

NEVER!

'Will we let them get away with it?'

NEVER!

Keep banging your pot! The rent men are on their way. Quick, quick, let's run to the window and hurl out flour bombs!

It's a bomb made with flour.

Flour, ya daftie. Like what you make cake and bread out of.

Now, let's march with Mrs Barbour's Army.

(Singing.) Oh we are women

And we are marching

Oh Bella Ciao Bella Ciao Bella Ciao Ciao Ciao

(Speaking.) Bang your pot!

(Singing.) Oh we are women

And we are marching

Oh Bella Ciao Ciao Ciao Ciao Ciao

(Speaking.) Here, you stand up on the chair like wur brother David has taken you up on his shooders tae keep you fae being trampled. Can you see? Can you see the whole of Argyle Street? Can you see all the huners of women? And now, now we're coming round to the Sherrif's Court and bang your pot it's John MacLean! And he's introducing Govan's very own Mrs Barbour!

Do you want to be Mrs Barbour this time?

Why not?

Well, you just carry on being me and mind you listen carefully so you can be Mrs Barbour next time.

Ready? Mrs Barbour!

'Comrades! Sisters! Brothers! Weans! Rent Strikers! / Hawd your whisht! Listen, to the songs that carry through the streets of Glasgow this day …'

> *MRS BARBOUR appears on a platform, speaking to the audience around her. GRACE fades as she speaks. MARY stays, watching her from her arm chair, caught between time.*

MRS BARBOUR: / Hawd your whisht! Listen, to the songs that carry through the streets of Glasgow this day. Men have stood here before and tomorrow will stand here again but today the streets of Glasgow flow with the Red Skirts of the Clyde. Twenty thousand women! Women like me from Govan. Some from Partick, Bridge of Weir, Kinning Park. Protestant women. Catholic women. Women with weans and grand weans and great grand weans. Women! Sisters! And brothers! Men from factories and ship yards from as far down the Clyde as Dalmuir and Clydebank stand here with us today, shoulder to shoulder all the way from here at the Sheriff's Court to Glasgow City Chambers. All traffic is at a stand still, all work on hold, the people's voice is strong and we will be heard! We demand that the government make illegal all increases of rent since this war began and that the town council proceed to erect new housing within reach of the working classes. And we will continue to fight until these demands are met. We fight them with bundles of wet washing and bread flour. With soup ladles and wooden spoons. We fight them with our pots and our pans. Our rolling pins and drums and bells and rattles. We fight them with our weans in our arms and the songs of the Clyde in our hearts. We struggle day to day for our daily bread. Living hugger mugger and while our husbands and sons and fathers and brothers are being slaughtered in Germany and France, our very basic needs are being slaughtered for the profit of a greedy few. Does the governing class of this country have no shame? Should not our grateful country protect their people's homes? Their people's needs? Their people's rights? Their basic rights of being alive? But such protection is not being given. And so I ask you now, will we let them get away with it? Say it with me: Never! I ask you: Will we stand for this tyranny? Never! For if the government does not defend our homes, we must defend them ourselves! If the government does not defend our basic needs, our basic rights for a life worth living, we must defend them ourselves! And so I ask you: Will we accept this injustice? Never! Then raise your voices and bang your pots and stamp your feet and sing with me, for we are women, and we are marching!

MARY, as her present day self, rises from her chair to sing. MRS BARBOUR disappears.

MARY: The words. I cannae remember the words.

MARY collapses.

SCENE ELEVEN
2015

RADIO: ... severe disruptions on the A739 Clyde Tunnel Expressway both north and south bound as the area prepares for a protest march causing road closures from Govan to Glasgow Green. Drivers are advised to consider alternative routes or allow more time for their journey. / Now for the weather. Cloudy with scattered showers across the ...

MARY lies on the floor. JOAN enters, turns off the radio and rushes to MARY.

JOAN: Oh God. Mary? Mary? Can you hear me? Mary?

MARY: No.

JOAN: Can you hear me?

MARY: No.

JOAN: Can you not hear me?

MARY: No.

JOAN: You can hear me?

MARY: Will you shut up?

JOAN: Oh thank Christ. Oh thank God. Here. Here, let me help you. Back into your chair. There you go. There. I'll get you a sip of water.

MARY: No.

JOAN: A glass of milk then? Will you take a wee drop of milk?

MARY: No.

JOAN: A cup of tea, I'll get you that cup of tea.

MARY: No.

JOAN: With a custard cream?

MARY: No.

JOAN: No?

MARY: No.

JOAN: No …

MARY: I'll take a Club Biscuit.

JOAN: Oh aunty Mary. Please forgive me.

MARY: No.

JOAN: Oh God.

JOAN's phone rings.

JOAN: Oh shite.

MARY: Answer it.

JOAN rejects the call. They look at each other.

MARY: What the hell are you doing here? Get out. Get out there into the world. Get out there and live your life.

JOAN: This is my life.

MARY: Some life.

JOAN: We have to make the best of what we've got.

MARY: That's not what Mrs Barbour would say.

JOAN: It's not like you to be talking about …

MARY: Named after her, so I was.

JOAN: You were named after her?

MARY: Mrs Mary Barbour. She would've said we've no need to just accept things the way they are. She'd've said if the government won't meet our basic rights for life worth living, well, we need to meet them ourselves.

JOAN: Are you alright?

MARY: No I'm not alright. I cannae get out of this chair. And I cannae make my own tea. And I cannae go to the toilet on my own. I cannae wash myself or dress myself. And I cannae see a hing except for my ain memories of my dead sister who, God help me, I never once spoke to for the last fifty years of her life.

JOAN: Did you never see us? We walked up this road every day to see if you were alright.

MARY: Oh I saw you. I stood at that window and watched you. But I promised myself I'd never speak to her again. And what have I got to show for it? A battered old saucepan and a wooden spoon. Just off you go now and leave me alone. I'll take a place in the home like they want me to and be a burden to you no more.

JOAN: I will not let you wait for death somewhere you're no more than a name on a check list. And that's not just because of a promise I made to my mother. It's not just because of the money I get for being your carer. It's not just because I care for you and love you – for all you drive me bananas. It's because no one who has the power to decide the future will ever give a bugger about the lives of you and me. And you don't deserve to have no one give a bugger about you. Neither did my mother. Neither do I. You're no burden, Mary. Not as long as I've got the space and the strength to stand beside you.

    Pause.

MARY: You wouldnae have enough room for my chair.

JOAN: My spare room's big enough for your bed and a wee sitabootery of your own.

MARY: You'd want me to change my wireless to wan of they fancy doohickeys with all they knobs and buttons.

JOAN: It'd be your room. You could do with it what you want.

Mischievously, MARY picks up the pan and spoon.

MARY: But what about these?

JOAN: Your chair. Your wireless. Your pan. Your spoon. In your hands. To do whatever it is you need to do. In your room looking out over the river Clyde. And you and me, well, we'll figure out what the way forward is for us both. For us all.

MARY: Well. If I do come, and I'm not saying I will, but if I do, you need to know, it will mainly be so that I can help you make a flour bomb should it ever be required.

A choir begin to sing Bella Ciao *– the women's liberation version of the song – keeping time with pots and pans. They are far away.*

JOAN: A flour bomb?

MARY: What's that?

JOAN: You tell me.

MARY: No, ya galoot, what is that singing?

JOAN: The radio's aff.

MARY: It's coming fae outside.

They listen. The singing is louder.

JOAN: Must be that parade I wis telling you about. The wan all they red traffic hingmies are out for.

MARY: Who are they?

JOAN goes to the window and looks out onto the streets below. The singing is louder now, the choir is in the auditorium.

JOAN: They're Mrs Barbour's Army!

MARY: Away with you, those women are dead and buried.

JOAN: Not these ones, Mary. They're alive and well. They're marching with drums and bells and pots and pans and holding an enormous sign saying 'Mrs Barbour's Army'. And another saying

'Women For Independence'. And another saying 'The Living Rent Campaign'. And other banners with words three foot high.

MARY: What do they say? What are they marching for?

JOAN: Liberty. Equality. Democracy.

MARY: Still?

JOAN: And there's a woman who looks just like my mother.

MARY: Grace?

JOAN: It's not her. Of course it's not her. But it looks like her when she was young. She's banging on her pot with a spoon and singing at the top of her voice.

The choir now fills the auditorium. People who have been sat watching the play, stand up one by one and join in the singing.

JOAN: And there are weans too. Waving flags and ringing bells. There's one wee girl high up on her big brother's shoulders. To keep her from being trampled I should think. She is waving up at us, Mary. She's waving and laughing. She can't be more than three or four! And she's singing, Mary!

MARY: The wean knows the words?

JOAN: Aye! She knows the words. And there's men too. Marching shoulder to shoulder with them. Hoy! Look! One young man's just joined in off the street. He's in amongst them all, right next to the boy with his wee sister up on his shoulders! They're laughing! He doesnae know the words to the songs so he's just singing la! La la la la la la!

MARY: Well two voices are always stronger than one.

JOAN: And everyone is smiling. Smiling and laughing and marching and banging their pots and their pans and…

MARY: Ach, woman, will you shut up and sing!

We sing.

The End.

Mary Barbour
(22 February 1875 – 2 April 1958)

A century ago the *Govan Press* reported remarkable scenes in connection with the 1915 rent strike:

> 'Headed by a band of improvised instruments, including tin whistles, hooters, and a huge drum, the procession aroused a good deal of interest. The majority carried large placards with the words: 'Rent Strikers. We're not Removing."

Men, women and children were involved; the women nicknamed 'Mrs Barbour's Army' in tribute to her leading role. Her capacity to mobilise working class families, especially women, to challenge the power of landlords and the state during the 1915 rent strike led to the passing of one of Europe's first rent restriction acts.

This article gives a brief narrative account of Mary Barbour's life. It also addresses some incorrect information in wide circulation. In particular, whilst Mary Barbour was many things, she was not Glasgow's first female councillor nor was she the city's first Labour woman councillor.

Background

Born in Kilbarchan in 1875, Mary Barbour was the third of seven children. Her father James Rough was a handloom weaver and later a carpet weaver. In 1887, the family moved to the village of Elderslie and Mary gained work as a thread twister, eventually becoming a carpet printer.

On 28 August 1896 she married David Barbour from Johnstone. Their first child David, born a few months after their marriage, died of meningitis at the age of ten months, a loss likely to have shaped her deep interest in health and housing issues. Although her husband also came from a textile family, David Barbour was a journeyman iron turner. His employment took them first to Dumbarton and then to Govan. They settled at 5 MacLeod Street, Govan (1901 Census), and later at 43 Ure Street (1911 Census). By 1911 David Barbour was a shipyard iron turner and they had two sons, James (11 years) and William (six years).

The Rent Strike 1915 and 'Mrs Barbour's Army'

Like many of her generation, Mary Barbour became active in a range of organisations. It seems she first joined the Kinning Park Co-operative Guild. This linked her to a platform campaigning against poverty and with specific policy demands to counter women's poverty such as maternity benefit, education, the vote and a national minimum wage. At the same time the Guild offered its members a structured political education. Mary also became involved in the Socialist Sunday School and the Independent Labour Party (ILP) and by 1914 had become the 'leading woman in Govan' within the new Glasgow Women's Housing Association formed to address Glasgow's greatest social problem, housing.

After the war started, the demands of war work and munitions brought an influx of workers into Glasgow. Property owners were swift to cash in and take the opportunity to raise rents in working class areas. The rent strike was the response and as historian James Smyth notes, Govan 'remained the major bulwark of the struggle'. One of the key players in Glasgow's radical politics, Helen Crawfurd, described the tactics used during the rent strike:

> 'Whenever the Bailiff's Officer appeared to evict a tenant, the woman in the passage immediately rang the bell, and the women came from all parts of the building. Some with flour, if baking, wet clothes, if washing, and other missiles. Usually the Bailiff made off for his life, chased by a mob of angry women.'

Mary Barbour was involved in every aspect of activities and Helen Crawfurd illustrated her leadership role:

> 'In Govan, on one occasion, where a woman had been persuaded by the House Factor to pay the increase, having been told that the other tenants had paid, Mrs Barbour got the men from the shipyards in Govan to come out on to the street where the House Factor's office was, and then went

up with the women and demanded a return of the money. On the Factor being shown the thousands of black-faced workers crowding the street, he handed it over.'

By November 1915 as many as 20,000 tenants were on rent strike in Glasgow and rent strike activity was spreading country-wide. The ILP activist, councillor and journalist Patrick Dollan writing as 'PJD' was tireless in publicising the spread of the strike, asserting in October 1915 that 'the Glasgow tenants are going to win'. The decision by a Partick factor to prosecute 18 tenants for non-payment of a rent increase brought the crisis to a head in Glasgow's Sheriff Court on 17 November 1915. Many of those in arrears were shipyard workers. There were strikes in support and deputations sent to the court whilst thousands demonstrated outside.

Amid news of imminent ministerial intervention, the cases were dismissed. Within a month the Rent Restriction Act restricting rents to their August 1914 level was in place and the rent strike's place in history was assured. James Smyth considers that 'it may well have been the most successful example of direct action ever undertaken by the Scottish working class'.

Mary Barbour's involvement in this struggle made her a local hero in Govan and much further afield. With further experience in the wartime Women's Peace Crusade behind her, the ILP acknowledged her powerful local presence in 1920, selecting her as one of their municipal candidates for the Fairfield ward in Govan.

Mary Barbour – 'Govan's First Woman Councillor'

The 1920 municipal election campaign was one of the first some women over 30 won the vote and Lloyd George had made the memorable post-war promise of 'Homes fit for Heroes'. Mary Barbour outlined a house-hold manifesto covering issues such as adulterated food, a municipal milk supply, abolition of wash-houses and the provision of public wash-houses and setting up child welfare centres where young children could play instead of having to remain in a tenement. She hoped that workers would press demands 'not only for better homes, but for a higher standard of living generally'.

She and four other women were elected to Glasgow Corporation, the first women elected in the city since the passing of the 1907 act allowing women to be elected and to act as town or county councillors.

It is widely believed, however, that Mary Barbour was Glasgow's first female councillor or at least the first woman Labour councillor. The entry for her in the *New Dictionary of National Biography (DNB)* states that 'she polled 4,701 votes, mainly from women, and was elected to Glasgow town council as their first Labour woman councillor'. This entry has contributed to the misapprehension and inevitably been repeated. The original source of the error seems likely to be Patrick Dollan whose *History of Kinning Park Cooperative Society Limited* published in 1923 described Mary Barbour as 'the first Co-operative woman elected to the council' and the 'first Labour woman to be elected to Glasgow Town Council'. The DNB sources include Dollan's book. A busy man's slip of the pen rewrote history.

At any rate, press reports and the Glasgow Corporation records make it clear that a group of five women were elected in 1920. In addition to Mary Barbour, Eleanor Stewart became ILP councillor for Maryhill whist Jessica Baird-Smith, Mary Bell and Mary Anderson Snodgrass were returned as Moderate councillors.

The Govan Press hailed Mary Barbour as 'Govan's first women councillor' but said that 'her work will be closely scrutinised'. A week later the paper reported that she emphasised the Labour Group 'were there for a particular purpose and that was to get the most out of the municipal administration of the city'. She had already found that the work was done in the committees and that 'the women had plenty of work to do and from now on would be in the Council Chambers every day'.

Mary Barbour served on the Corporation until stepping down in 1931. In 1924 she marked other milestones for women in public office when she became both a Bailie and a magistrate. Her party colleague Patrick Dollan told the press that 'he was pleased to have the distinction of introducing the first fully fledged woman magistrate of the City of Glasgow'.

Her focus on families continued and in November 1926 she saw the opening of the new Elder Park Child Welfare Association. At the opening Mary Barbour informed the audience that the Clinic 'was not merely a child welfare centre, but an institution for 'mother-craft' – and 'father-craft', too'. Her support for Glasgow's first birth control clinic was more controversial. This went against the voting record of her Socialist MP colleagues, none of whom had supported the Birth Control Enabling Bill in 1922. The Glasgow Women's Welfare and Advisory Clinic opened in August 1926 at 51 Govan Road to give advice to married women on family planning.

In 1931 she opted to stand down as a councillor at the age of 56 stating that she felt 'the difficulties ahead required young and strenuous fighters'. Eight women were elected to Glasgow Corporation in 1931 (7.2 per cent), two Moderate and six Labour. The *Glasgow Herald* reported that 'all the Labour women candidates met with success'. It can be safely assumed that Mary Barbour would have been both selected and elected had she stood again.

Conclusion

Outstanding questions remain over Mary Barbour's career, over why she stood down as councillor, and a need for more information on the campaigns that she was involved in. In that sense I am still looking for Mary Barbour.

When she died in 1958 Bailie Jack Davis wrote an obituary for the *Govan Press* noting that:

> 'There are women in Govan today who think of Mrs Mary Barbour as one of the great leaders of the Labour Movement who truly represented its spirit and purpose, and I am inclined to agree with them. … Mrs Barbour has been out of the limelight of

public affairs in this city for many years now but there never was a more revered and loved local leader than she was in the heyday of her active life.'

The obituary also mentions that 'women voluntarily took on hand to do the housework of Mrs Barbour to enable her to devote herself fully to the service of the people' – a practical and unusual tribute. Direct and forthright, Mary Barbour emerges as a strong, energetic and convincing campaigner who helped to make the world a different place from the one that was in war torn crisis in 1915. Her role in the rent strike was crucial to its success and won her fame. In elected office she sought to implement the ILP and Co-operative household agenda. She is worthy of being remembered – and of being commemorated by a statue.

Catriona Burness
Catriona Burness is a writer, researcher and campaigner working with the Remember Mary Barbour Association to secure a permanent and physical memorial to the pioneering social activist and Labour political leader. She has written and published extensively on women and Scottish politics.

The Remember Mary Barbour Association aims to create a lasting memorial to one of Glasgow's greatest heroes. For more information or to donate please see: http://remembermarybarbour.wordpress.com or email info@remembermarybarbour.com

The Red Clyde

Memories are important. For those committed to radical social change Clydeside's forty hours strike of 1919 was remembered as a moment of unfulfilled revolutionary potential. Tom Bell, an iron moulder from Glasgow's east end, recalled the strike as the time when the Red Clyde became central to the hopes of workers across Britain – a strike 'spreading rapidly across the rest of the country and assuming all the possibilities of a general political strike'. Another participant, Willie Gallacher, later described it as having all the potential of a 'rising' and recalled the anti-war poet Siegfried Sassoon as among those who travelled up to the Clyde from London 'with intense hatred of the social system responsible for the past black [war] years he came to Glasgow to welcome a change whatever course it took'. This assessment of Red Clydeside's potential for social transformation was also shared, from a different perspective, by employers and government. Red like the Paris Commune of 1871. Red like Russia in 1917.

The forty hours strike was remarkable in many ways. It involved hundreds of thousands of workers. Yet it was (mainly) an unofficial strike and was conducted without strike pay. Its objective was not immediate financial gain but to enforce a major shortening of hours – seeking to prevent the return of mass unemployment after the war and to provide jobs for returning servicemen and for the generation of young women discharged from the munitions industry. It spread from the shipyards of the Clyde to the coalfields of Lanarkshire and Fife, to the ports and engineering works of Rosyth, Leith, Dundee and Aberdeen – and then on to South Wales and London and was accompanied by a parallel strike in Belfast. On Clydeside it involved the setting up of neighbourhood based strike committees, the withholding of rents, the mobilisation of apprentices and young women on mass pickets and, after the occupation of Glasgow by military forces from the south, women taking the leading part in defying troops guarding workplace entrances.

It was a mass strike that transformed communities and attitudes – but it was only possible because it drew on prior experience and organisation built up over two decades.

1. Clydeside: heavy industry, slums and poverty

At the beginning of the 20th century Clydeside contained Britain's biggest concentration of heavy industry: 500,000 workers were employed in shipbuilding, railway construction, iron and steel founding and coalmining. Wages were generally lower than those in England. Employment was much less secure as demand rose and fell for ships, railway equipment and engines. Between 1903 and 1905 and again between 1907 and 1910 output declined by 40 per cent and employment by almost as much. Workers sought the cheapest accommodation in face of this insecurity. Over two-thirds of families lived in one or two rooms in grim ill-ventilated tenements, often six or seven to a room. One child in six was dead before its sixth birthday, about the worst record for child mortality in Western Europe.

Trade union organisation was patchy: quite strong in engineering and shipbuilding, weak in services industries, textiles and light engineering. The giant Coats thread combine in Paisley banned unions among its mainly female workforce. The Singer Sewing Machine plant, employing 12,000 in Clydebank, also refused to recognise trade unions for its women workers. On the other hand, the booms and slumps of pre-war employment placed a premium on using the periods of rapid expansion to retrieve lost conditions and push up wages. This seems to have been one reason for the strength of a workplace-based shop-stewards movement across Clydeside's engineering and shipbuilding. The brutality of living conditions and the confrontational nature of industrial relations also saw the development of a relatively strong socialist movement. This was led by the Independent Labour Party (ILP), with its weekly paper *Forward*, along with significant influence from Marxists such as John Maclean of the British Socialist Party (BSP) and the syndicalists of the Socialist Labour Party who help sustain the massive but ultimately unsuccessful strike by the women workers at Singers in 1912. Overall, however, the political representation of Labour was weaker in Scotland, with only two Labour MPs against over 30 in England, and Scottish society remained strongly dominated by its elite of industrialists and landowners and by a Church of Scotland still wedded to quite reactionary loyalties to Scotland's Protestant heritage and opposition to the Irish Catholic immigrants who made up over a quarter of Clydeside's population.

War transformed this situation. Clydeside became Britain's major centre for both warship building and for general munitions production. Workers poured in – and landlords pushed up rents at the same time as the price of food and other necessities also rose sharply. The government sought to maximise war production, and eliminate any potential for disruption, by entering agreements with trade union leaderships that suspended previously negotiated agreements on working practices and, very soon afterwards, made strikes illegal. In consequence, as wartime hardships increased, the 'unofficial movement', made up of shop-stewards and workplace representatives, was thrust into the forefront of defending workers and their families. For the first time workers, if organised, had unparalleled power in the workplace. But using that power was illegal – so leadership was increasingly taken by those whose socialist and anti-war convictions made them willing to defy the law.

The development of Red Clyde went in three phases. The first was defensive. The objective was to maintain real wages, defend workplace rights and, in the communities, take action against rising rents. But it was not overtly anti-war or political. This period lasted through 1915 and into 1916. The second was from early 1917 till summer 1918. This period saw an escalation of strike action and a rising challenge to the war culminating in the illegal mass strike accompanying the 80,000 strong 1918 May Day demonstration. At this stage the politics of the leaders, and the wider international situation, was beginning to create a significant though still minority base for socialist politics. The third period began at the end of the war. The unofficial movement, led by the Clyde Workers Committee but with the support of the Scottish Trade Union Congress, sought to prevent the return of mass unemployment and to maintain Labour's strong bargaining position by forcing a drastic reduction of hours from 54 to 40. The government's response then led to the development of much more widespread support for socialist politics across Clydeside.

2. Defending Workplace Rights: Defending Communities

Within four months of the outbreak of war, in December 1914, engineering workers revived an earlier wage de-mand and called for a 2d an hour increase to compensate for inflation. In face of wartime prohibitions on strikes and the failure of union officials to pursue the claim, they cre-ated the Clyde Labour Withholding Committee (CLWC) made up workplace representatives from across the Clyde and imposed an overtime ban. In February 1915 this dis-pute developed into an all-out strike when one of the big-gest engineering works on Glasgow's south side, Weirs of Cathcart, employed American engineers at much higher rates of pay. Eventually the government intervened and employers were pushed into agreeing a partial increase in March 1915.

This first encounter showed the potential of unofficial organisation and established the credentials of its leaders, mostly members of left-wing parties who had taken a generally anti-war position: Jim Messer, Secretary of the CLWC, of the ILP, Willie Gallacher, its chair, from Albion Motors and a member of the BSP and other leading stewards such as Arthur McManus, a member of the SLP from Weirs, and John Muir also a member of the SLP, from Barr and Strouds. The government's response was to enact the Munitions Act giving employers and government officials much more direct powers to fine and imprison those seen to be disrupting the war effort. The result was renewed conflict and defiance. In August 1915 the managers of the giant Fairfields shipyard in Govan dismissed two workers for not working hard enough. When the Fairfield shop-stewards organised a protest strike they were arrested and imprisoned under the Munitions Act. In turn Govan Trades Council called for wider strike action in a dispute that dragged on until the release of the shipwrights in early November and saw the CLWC re-launched as the Clyde Workers Committee (CWC).

Over the same period rent strikes also began against landlords seeking to profit from the new demand for housing. Average increases ran at around 20 per cent. The first of the rent strikes were in the west of the city in the tenements housing workers from the shipyards of Govan, Partick and Scotstoun. These started in August 1915. By October-November large areas of the north and the east of the city were also refusing to pay rents. Organisation was provided by existing local tenants associations whose leaders were usually also members of the ILP or, like John Maclean, of the BSP. In many cases the organisers were women associated with Suffragist movements who had taken personally taken an anti-war position: Mary Barbour, Agnes Dollan and Helen Crawfurd. What made the rent strikes particularly important was the high level of local community organisation they required. Each household had to be persuaded to take the risky step of withholding rent and tenants had to be mobilised very quickly to fend off sheriff officers seeking to enforce evictions.

Resistance came to a head in November when an attempt was made to use the Sheriff Court to secure direct deductions of rent arrears from workers' wages. This immediately brought together the unofficial movement in shipyards and munitions works and local tenants' organisations. The scale of the mass demonstration on 17 November forced the government to take immediate steps to legislate a freeze on rents at the pre-war level.

The climax of this first stage followed quickly – the humiliation of Lloyd George on Christmas Day 1915. By autumn 1915 the government and employers were seeking to expand war production by drafting semi-skilled and unskilled workers, principally women, into work previously undertaken by skilled craftsmen without paying the skilled rate. The pro-war union leaderships went along with these proposals. The CWC sought to organise resistance – demanding that the government stop private profiteering by taking war production into public ownership and paying all workers the rate for the job. Lloyd George, then Minister of Munitions, together with union leaders from London, came up to Clydeside to make a direct appeal to workers in the main munitions works. The CWC persuaded workers to refuse these meetings and instead insisted the Lloyd George hear their own alternative proposals. Then on Christmas Day they packed the final mass meeting in Glasgow's St Andrews Hall. Three thousand shop stewards assembled to prevent Lloyd George putting his own proposals. The ILP's paper *Forward*, defied wartime censorship to publish the proceedings in full.

The government response was immediate. *Forward* and John Maclean's paper, *The Vanguard*, were suppressed. On 5 January conscription was announced – a threat to all workers deemed not essential – and team of top level civil servants came up to Clydeside to hold negotiations on a firm by firm basis that offered concessions and assurances on the dilution process.

Against this background the CWC waged a losing battle to mobilise support for its demands. The government provoked a partial strike that enabled them to deport most of the leading shop steward members of the CWC in March 1916. The leaders, Gallacher and John Muir were arrested under the Defence of the Realm Act for the publishing the CWC weekly, *The Worker*, and imprisoned till February 1917.

So this first stage saw workers demonstrate their potential power. It also saw the exercise of this power to create new links between workplaces and the community. But the demands were essentially economic and defensive. Though the leaders were almost all anti-war, the government was still able to use patriotic appeals to isolate them. The wider political demands of the CWC for nationalisation failed secure a mass response.

3. Anti-war sentiment begins to gain the upper hand

The second stage saw a widening of the scope of trade union action to semi-skilled and unskilled workers and a deepening political involvement. Despite the decapitation of the CWC in March 1916, the spring and summer saw a spate of strikes outside shipbuilding and engineering – mainly about trade union rights among previously unorganised workers. In March April 1916, 3,000 printing workers, mainly women, struck work to enforce a union closed shop. In June and July 1916 women workers in flax spinning, clothing and laundries struck work in a series of strikes for trade union rights and wage increases. By 1917 the number of days lost to strike action far exceeded those in 1915 – with all sections of shipbuilding and engineering entering a succession of strikes to secure 'war bonuses' that kept pace with inflation.

Over these months the political grip of the pro-war establishment also began to slip. A succession of events played their part. April 1916 saw the Irish Rising. This initially secured little or no support within the labour movement in Scotland but the brutality of its suppression, particular the execution of the labour leader James Connolly, created an unease that spread well beyond Clydeside's large Irish community. Conscription and the scale of war casualties also brought an increasing questioning of the war. In June the same group of women suffragists who had given leadership in the rent strikes, Helen Crawfurd, Agnes Dollan and Mary Barbour, organised a Women's Peace Conference in Glasgow from which developed the Women's Peace Crusade. In 1917 the overthrow of the Tsar in February, combined with the Zimmerwald peace movement of the old Second International of socialist parties, began to create a new international context for strong anti-war element within the ILP. In December 1917 news arrived of the Bolshevik revolution in Russia and its slogans of peace, bread and land. Meetings many thousands strong were addressed by leaders of the ILP and the BSP. John Maclean was appointed Soviet Consul in Glasgow in February 1918.

These events coincided with a new much bigger strike wave spreading through the munitions sector and across shipbuilding. Clydeside again became the major focus for government intervention. On 15 December 1917 the Ministry of Munitions Clyde Labour Report warned: 'the early months of 1918 may reveal industrial action with a view to the achievement of political ends for the ending of war conditions'. Opposition to the Manpower Bill, for the 'comb out' of conscripts from industry, brought anger on a scale equal to that in December 1915. When Auckland Geddes, the minister responsible for conscription, visited Clydeside in January 1918 he was faced with a mass meeting of workplace representatives every bit as rowdy as that which met Lloyd George. Now, however, opposition was far more politically focused – with resolutions passed in explicit support of the peace moves being made by the new Soviet government in Russia.

The government responded by concessions on the wages front combined with a massive propaganda initiative. A special section of the Ministry of Information was established to deal with Clydeside unrest. Newspapers were fed with government-inspired stories and government-sponsored meetings were held in every workshop. Massive repression was directed against anyone speaking out against the war – both in terms of the arrest of leaders on sedition charges and the detailed conscription of known supporters. Gallacher was arrested and in April John Maclean. None of this, however, sufficed to turn the tide. In February 1918 the Glasgow Trades Council decided to organise the 1918 May Day during the working week – effectively an illegal general strike. The government was unable to do anything to stop it. At least 80,000 attended. Motions were passed for the release of John Maclean, in support of the Russian Revolution, for the withdrawal of British intervention troops and for the immediate initiation of peace negotiations. Two weeks later Maclean delivered his famous speech from the dock at the High Court in Edinburgh:

'I wish no harm to any human being, but I, as one man, am going to exercise my freedom of speech. No human being on the face of the earth, no government is going to take from me my right to speak, my right to protest against wrong, my right to do everything that is for the benefit of mankind. I am not here, then, as the accused; I am here as the accuser of capitalism dripping with blood from head to foot.'

This second period therefore saw a far more politicised movement – particularly in terms of opposition to war. It consolidated the leadership of the CWC and the Glasgow Trades Council, then holding monthly meetings attended by upwards of five hundred branch delegates. It also placed Glasgow at the centre of a network of contacts that spread across industrial Scotland and to other centres of anti-war and socialist resistance in England and Wales. But it remained, within the overall population of Clydeside, a minority movement in terms of socialist objectives. This was demonstrated in the December 1918 general election when government-backed Coalition candidates won all but one of the seats in Glasgow. Even though owners of office property still possessed extra votes and the politicised younger age group of women were excluded, the scale of victory indicated that politically a majority of working families still supported the existing order. Only in the shipbuilding constituency of Govan did a socialist candidate get elected: Neil McLean, leader of the 'Hands off Russia' campaign.

4. The General Strike of 1919

As already noted, the 1919 general strike had limited and very practical objectives: a forty hour week to permit the re-absorption of servicemen and munitions workers into the peacetime labour force. It was called by the CWC, the Glasgow Trades Council and the Scottish Trades Union Congress (STUC) but was not supported by the generally pro-war leaders of the main unions.

On the first day, Monday, support was limited to perhaps 30,000 workers in the main shipyards and engineering work. But then it spread rapidly. Critical here were mass pickets made up largely of apprentices and young women. By Wednesday the power station supplying current to industry in Glasgow was shut down and the Lanarkshire and Fife coalfields came out. At this point, after some initial complacency, local employers and the government became seriously alarmed. The police were unable to stop the mass pickets. Demands were made for military intervention. In London Bonar Law, Deputy Prime Minister, telephoned Lloyd George at the Paris peace conference to say the King was 'in a funk about the labour situation' and demanding Lloyd George's immediate return in case of 'revolution'. On Friday some 30,000 strikers assembled at the City Chambers to call for the Lord Provost to intervene with the government. The demonstration was met by a police charge. The resulting melee was used as the pretext for city's occupation by 12,000 troops that night.

Most accounts of the general strike end the story there – with tanks on the streets and machine guns in George Square. But the most significant part of the strike was yet to come. The strike did not end. The conference called by the STUC on the Sunday overwhelmingly voted for the strike's extension. On the streets the main purpose of the military was to halt the mass pickets. Soldiers with fixed bayonets were stationed at road junctions, bridges and outside main workplaces. It was here that the organisational steps taken at the beginning of the strike came into play. Willie Gallacher, as chair of the organising committee, had insisted on the establishment of area strike committees and the withholding of rents – bringing into play existing neighbourhood organisations. On the Monday, women, many with young children, were reported as fronting the pickets and defying the soldiers.

On the following Wednesday the assessment of the STUC was that the situation was moving in their favour as the supportive strikes erupted in England and South Wales. By then transport had been halted in London and railways paralysed across much of the south and west. With the electricians threatening the halting of the capital's power supplies that night, the Cabinet met to decide the measures to be announced in the King's speech. Reversing previous policy to cut expenditure and deflate the economy, the Cabinet decided on a massive programme of house building and the extension of health and welfare provisions, measures later described by Lloyd George later as 'insurance against Bolshevism'. The same meeting also ordered the use of the Defence of the Realm Act against the London electricians and mobilised the army to break the transport strikes in the capital.

Only a week later did the Strike Committee in Glasgow call for an orderly return to work. The Ministry of Labour report for the same day warned 'the Joint Committee of the Clyde Strike instructed the workers to resume on Wednesday, 12 February [...] The strike is said to be only postponed until it can be reconvened on a national basis'. The final issue of the Strike Bulletin, which by then had a daily circulation of 20,000, was defiant:

> 'If we go back to work, we do so only to change our tactics. ... The strike already then has burst the infamous 47 hours proposal [referring to the capitulation by the employers in Belfast]. As a result of our agitation workers across the country realise that the 40 hours week is the one practicable remedy for unemployment ... the barriers of craft have gone over in this conflict, and, henceforth we fight as workers, irrespective of trade or occupation. ... nevermore will one section be used against another ... The strike has taught us our power; has developed our capacity; has shown us where our organisation is weak. The knowledge we have gained will not be wasted.'

The employers moved very warily – the main employers association instructing members not to attempt to penalise local strike leaders. Nationally the government was equally cautious. Ministers were immediately faced with the demand from Britain's biggest union, the miners, that the mines be permanently nationalised. Rather than face a further confrontation, they played for time and appointed a Commission.

On Clydeside military intelligence reported: 'there is no doubt that a great number of workmen are very much unsettled and the greatest importance is attached to proper counter propaganda'. Four months later government ministers agreed a massive programme of anti-socialist propaganda – funded half and half from the Treasury and major employers. The prime movers were the Glasgow industrialist William Weir and the Minister of Labour, Robert Horne, a Glasgow MP. £200,000 was allocated (£500 million in today's money) for the covert syndicalisation of newspaper articles, the production of school syllabuses and the sponsorship of books in civics and economics.

May Day 1919 was also held on a working day on Clydeside. The number of striking workers exceeded those in 1918. Resolutions were passed for the release of arrested strike leaders and for the immediate withdrawal of British intervention troops from Soviet Russia. In the autumn local elections in Glasgow there was a massive swing to Labour across the city – with the Chair of Glasgow Trades Council, Emmanuel Shinwell, just out of prison, receiving a 62 per cent vote.

Red Clyde was now firmly established in the mind of the government and, more important, in the minds of ordinary workers and their families. Looking back, Tom Bell and Gallacher saw 1919 as a time of unfulfilled potential for much wider social change. Yet attitudes had been transformed. Previous years had seen the slow building of solidarity and organisation across workplaces and communities. In 1919 local communities had witnessed military occupation to break a strike for full employment and re-impose an economic regime that depended on unemployment. By the time of next general election in 1922 Labour Party and Communist candidates, including a number of the strike leaders, captured the great bulk of Clydeside seats.

John Foster

John Foster is currently Secretary of Marx Memorial Library in London. He previously taught at the Universities of the West of Scotland, Strathclyde and Cambridge. He is the author of *Class Struggle and the Industrial Revolution* (1974) and, jointly with Charles Woolfson, *The Politics of the UCS Work-in* (1986), *Track Record*, 1988 (on the Caterpillar occupation) and *Paying for the Piper* (1996) on industrial relations in the North Sea oil industry. He lives in Govan.

The Other Mary

There's a modest section of wall on the Scottish Parliament building in Edinburgh, facing onto the Canongate at the foot of the Royal Mile, which is given over to twenty-six chiselled inscriptions. It's the symbolic lungs of the parliament, breathing intent into that place and what unfolds within it.

There's Burns (twice), of course, 'for a that and a that'. There's John Muir and Edwin Morgan, Andrew Fletcher of Saltoun and Sir Walter Scott, Alasdair Gray and Hugh MacDiarmid (also twice). All magnificent men, of course.

Only one inscription on this wall is by a woman. And it's a great weary sigh.

> Oh dear me the warld's ill divided
> them that works the hardest are aye wi least provided
> but I maun bide contented dark days or fine
> there's nae much pleasure livin affen ten and nine

The song is *Oh Dear Me*, also known as *The Jute Mill Song*, and that woman, that writer, thinker, shifter, spinner, fiddler, feminist and socialist activist is Mary Brooksbank.

On December 15th 1897, with the boats iced in at the harbour and dock work thin on the ground as a result, Mary Soutar, as she began life, came into the world at 29 Shiprow, off Union Street in Aberdeen, one of the dankest city slums of its day. She weighed just four and a half pounds and was born blind. Though the doctor said it was a blessing that she probably wouldn't live, nevertheless he gifted her mother some eye drops and the only electric torch in the whole neighbourhood. And, as it happens, daily checking her eyesight with that new fangled light, one April morning, when the wee girl was 14 months old, Rosie Soutar noted a flicker of response in her daughter's eyes. She ran helter-skelter down to the coal boat the Alice Taylor, where her man Sandy was working as a shoreside labourer, yelling 'Come on, come on! My bairn sees!'

Some 67 years later, in a recorded interview with Hamish

Henderson for the School of Scottish Studies Archive, Mary herself would intone wryly, 'Here I am. And I'm seeing too much sometimes now'.

Rosie Soutar's wee lassie was to see much in her later life which outraged her. And, like Mary Barbour, the Glasgow Rent Strike activist of 1915, and countless other women before her and since, she would refuse to be quiet about it. Instead, Mary Brooksbank would articulate a piercing awareness of inequality in her poetry and songs. She would document the lives and celebrate the spirit of impoverished working people and oppose injustice directly through collective action against the dreaded Means Test Inspectors. And she would pursue the cause of human dignity via demands for living wages, public health and decent housing. Three times she'd end up in Perth Jail on account of speaking her truth clearly about what she saw.

I first encountered *Oh Dear Me* in a chilly Victorian classroom at Boroughmuir High School in Edinburgh in 1997. Every Monday night for two years I attended an Adult Learning Project evening class called 'Women and Folksong', which was led by the Edinburgh singer, songwriter and lifelong community activist Eileen Penman. At the time I had just started in post as a Children's Rights Worker with Scottish Women's Aid and I was heavily involved in campaigning around essential support services for children and women fleeing domestic abuse. I was, also, newly enchanted with the world of Scottish folk music, and the way it interacted with contemporary political and social issues. I hung out at Dick Gaughan gigs and learned the words to Hamish Henderson's *Freedom Come All Ye*.

That late nineties evening class was stapped full of women breathing out the daily stresses of our working lives. We numbered child protection social workers, welfare rights advisors, youth workers, palliative care nurses and community activists. All of us were seeking a kind of connection with one other, as well as a connection with songs that spoke of the struggles and spirit of women in other times and places, including those we could call our own cultural ancestors. The social and health care jobs most of us inhabited were precisely those that Mary Brooksbank fought for, from a time in which infant mortality in many of Scotland's industrial towns and cities was close to twenty per cent, and the NHS and the Welfare State were but a socialist dream.

The act of singing in community with others in that draughty old school was deeply physically, emotionally and politically restorative for all of us. For me, it is still. Indeed it's why I sing. Mary Brooksbank knew this feeling too. In a poem called, simply, *Singing*, she'd write:

> There's nothing that can daunt me lang
> Gin I have power tae sing a sang

Mary's friend, the late folk singer Ray Fisher described her as 'one of the quiet giants, although she stood just over five foot tall'. Her tiny stature was matched by an unassuming manner of speaking too, one it's possible to hear still nearly 40 years after her death, courtesy of the online Tobar An Dualchais Archive at The University of Edinburgh. And there, in a 1965 conversation with Hamish Henderson, she'd observe, 'many's a time I've sung tae keep myself fae greetin. But still you get through it. Singing is a fine antidote to any trouble you have.'

I know this to be true.

I love the musicality of voices, in speech as well as song. The intonation, tone and pace of a voice betrays a lot about a person. And Mary's voice, swathed in 1960s tape hiss, in between distorted glitches and clicks, is neither hectoring nor declaratory. It has a sweet cup of tea ordinariness and warmth to it. Yet there's an unmistakable mischief, principle and purpose in it too, as she distills her life into story nuggets that she's obviously polished and tended in repeated tellings.

She speaks in one recording, for example, of how her parents married at Factory Street in Inverness in 1895, and spent their entire life savings of 30 shillings on a fabulous three day wedding stramash and a fancy pair of black patent leather shoes for Rosie. She tells of how they walked right after, penniless and barefoot, Sandy with the laces of his new wife's good shoes tied round his neck to keep them from the gravel, all the way from Inverness to Aberdeen.

There's something about the innocence and determination of her mother and father as a young couple that strikes me now as an intimation of her own life, of having next to nothing yet sharing it round, of eking every sliver of joy and celebration out of what you have, and of journeying on in resolute hope of something better. Indeed, she'd later capture this aspect of her own person in a poem called *The Robin*, which closes:

If you can whistle
that has sae little
then so can I.

And, though she was by her own account 'just a wee woman, the kind they used to burn', my, she could whistle.

She could whistle and she could see. And in her clearsighted-ness and her need to speak out about what she saw, she had lineage.

Mary's father Alexander, or Sandy, was one of the founder members of the dockers union in Aberdeen. Mary would write later in her poem *The Docker* about a man just like him, with his 'shouthers skint and feet sae sair'.

The Soutar household kitchen was a hotbed of organisational activity, through which many of the leading Scottish union activists of the era passed, talking and planning, singing and telling stories. Sandy visited Edinburgh for meetings convened by the Transport Workers Union and the Marxist Social Democratic Federation, where he met renowned socialist and Irish republican activist James Connolly.

In 1909 the Soutars flitted by boat from Aberdeen to Pump Close just off The Overgate in Dundee, before moving on to the slums of Blackness Road. Dock work for men like Sandy was erratic and ill-paid. So Rosie took up work in the jute mills which dominated the city's industrial landscape.

As a thirteen-year old schoolgirl, under the permitted legal working age, Mary herself started as a bobbin shifter at The Baltic Jute Mill. When she wasn't working twelve hour shifts, she was, in her own words, as the only surviving girl of the family, 'ae the wee mother'. She looked after four younger brothers in order that their mother Rosie could work. Five other Soutar bairns had not made it past infancy.

Seventy per cent of Dundee women and girls worked in the jute industry in that year of 1911 and two thirds of the total mill workforce were female. Indeed, young men were often laid off at eighteen years old before they were entitled to a full adult wage. Women were cheaper labour. Consequently the city had the highest rate of employment in the whole country for married women.

In December of that same year, Mary witnessed massed political action for the first time. The Dundee Carter's Strike was called in demand of a shilling a week in wages for the men who carted the jute bales through the city's streets and down to the docks for lucrative export. Mary, whilst running out to fetch her father his bread and tea, met a crowd of cart men singing The Red Flag. When, later on in the kitchen, she hummed the melody and her mother wondered aloud at where she'd picked up such a 'Protestant tune', it was Sandy Soutar who delighted in informing them both of its political intent.

At 6am, the morning after the sinking of the Titanic in April 1912, Mary started her first official job: alongside her own mother at the city's Kydd's Mill. Within months, she was caught up in her first workplace strike action. It was led by a young woman she'd recall only as 'the lassie wi the green felt hat', a woman who could whistle too. And it was with a literal sharp shrill blow that she'd mobilise the predominantly female workforce from mill to mill across the city in protest against the provisions of the freshly implemented National Insurance Act. The Act required defined classes of working people to pay 6d insurance against the possibility of future unemployment or illness. It was a fee unaffordable to young apprentice workers and to women, many of whom were the sole breadwinners of their households, and whose wages were less than fifty per cent of their male counterparts.

The strike was one of over a hundred called in the Dundee jute mills between 1889 and 1914, most led by women workers. And it was a glorious success, securing a fifteen per cent pay rise to offset the impact of the new legislation.

Fifty-six years later, in her sole poetry and lyric collection *Sidlaw Breezes*, Mary would include the text for one of the 1912 strike songs:

We are out for higher wages
As we have a right to do
And we'll never be content
Til we get our ten per cent
For we have a right to live as well as you

She would in retrospect, in her autobiography *No Sae Lang Syne*, describe this as her earliest lesson in 'class warfare'.

When she was 16, and working by then at the Craigie Mill in the city's east end, Mary learned to spin, first on a single frame and then a double. Though it's not clear at what point in her life Mary wrote many of her poems and songs, her earliest working experiences in the mills certainly informed them. *The Spinner's Wedding*, for example, gives a sense of the rebelliousness, confidence and collective power of the mill women she worked alongside. In this industrial environment, even the celebration of a marriage could become mischievously subversive:

The shifters they're a dancing
The spinners singing tae
The gaffer's standing watching
But theres' nothing he can dae

The song closes with what I regard as Mary's trademark blend of both pragmatic realism (even a touch of fatalism) and a dogged hopeful resolve, a quality it shares with its jute mill sister song *Oh Dear Me*.

Ye'll no make muckle siller
Nae maitter hoo ye try
But hoard ye love and loyalty
That's what money cannae buy

The WWI years and those immediately following radicalised Mary. In 1922, she joined the Communist Party of Great Britain, as one of its earliest female members. That year marked also her first criminal conviction, along with around twenty others, on a Breach of the Peace charge for breaking the two minute Armistice silence. She was sentenced to 40 days in Perth Jail and would recall later the uplifting sound of the crowds who gathered daily outside the prison to sing in protest.

Following Mary's brief imprisonment, her mother Rosie encouraged her to seek a better life away from Dundee and the mills. Mary explains, 'My mother put me into service for a period, tried to make me genteel, you know. She gave me a lovely outfit but it didnae suit me. It was the worst thing she could've did for I saw right away the contrast between their homes and ours, the gentry's homes and ours'.

She worked briefly in Wormit in North Fife as a domestic servant for one of the jute manufacturers whose mansions populated the Tay Coast, and also briefly in The Borders, before moving to service in Glasgow's Kelvinside. There she met her future husband Ernest Brooksbank, a skilled tailor to trade. It was in Glasgow, during a six month stay, that she attended Scottish Labour College lectures by the most revered socialist organiser and orator of the era, John Maclean, not long before his own untimely death on St Andrew's Day 1923.

Mary and Ernest returned to Dundee and married on October 3rd, 1924.

Throughout the mid to late 1920s Mary continued to agitate for labour rights and basic social services. Around the time of the General Strike, she was arrested again for heckling at a Town Council meeting regarding the 1921 Unemployment Insurance Act. The Act's 'genuinely seeking work' clause forced the unemployed, who numbered around twenty per cent of the adult population, to move constantly in search of work that did not exist, simply in order to prove their entitlement to dole payments.

According to Mary's own account, the authorities attempted to explain away her protestations by questioning her sanity. They placed her under a three week psychiatric supervision, citing the recent death of her younger brother as premise for a supposed nervous breakdown. Her grief was real, of course. But the Judge in her case found her health and judgment utterly sound, and the charge against her was found Not Proven.

Meantime, Mary, along with her mother Rosie, had taken up joint care of her late brother's infant son, Fred.

The heckling charge wasn't her last brush with the law. In 1931, following a demonstration in central Dundee, organised by the National Unemployed Workers Movement, Mary was convicted of sedition and sent to Perth Jail for a three month term. During her time away, The Railway Women's Guild of Perth brought her regular food parcels and ten thousand people signed a petition for her release. Even the Prison Governor himself, in admiration at her conviction and intelligence, loaned her a book on women and politics.

On her release, Mary put her energies towards developing The Working Women's Guild of Dundee, within the framework of the local Communist Party. Its aim was to encourage broader participation of women, and to support them in developing vital new political skills such as chairing and organising meetings and public speaking. The Guild lobbied internally to ensure that public health and social housing had the highest priority in the party's campaigns. And externally they promoted fundraising concerts for the unemployed and for International Class War Prisoners Aid and lobbied successfully for improvements to Poorhouse conditions in the city. The women crafted also an early bell system to warn of unannounced visitations by the much loathed Means Test Inspectors. Mary Barbour and the Glasgow rent strikers had done much the same a decade before in dodging WW1 Rent Collectors. And nearly a hundred years after that The Glasgow Girls would organise a collective watch system to head off Immigration Department dawn raids against failed asylum seekers in the city. These collective efforts map a century of small scale, localised, woman-powered solidarity.

The success of the Guild, growing to over 300 members within a couple of years, made Mary a target of resentment within the local Communist Party. Not only was she ardent in her advocacy for women, she was outspoken in her criticism of Stalin (she'd later write of his 'sorry stink'). She believed also in a kind of political solidarity that transcended strict party boundaries. And so, when asked to stand for election against Dundee Labour Councillor D R Kidd, whom she deemed 'a good fighter' for housing rights, she refused to split the left wing vote.

Mary's feminist principles and her pragmatic socialism did not fit neatly within the patriarchal strictures of the contemporary Communist Party of Great Britain. She was inevitably expelled in 1932 for indiscipline and factionalism. More than thirty years later, she'd reflect, again in conversation with Hamish Henderson, that: 'The women, they were making the Communist Party, you know. They chaired meetings for the Communist Party, went on deputations. And we got things done, we got better treatment for the old people, and the inhabitants of the poor houses, it was them. We got concessions and we did good work.'

By the time she reached her early forties during the early years of WWII, Mary's reputation for radical workplace and civic activism rendered her unable to find employment in any of Dundee's jute mills. She recognised that she was a 'marked' woman. Under pressure from the Unemployment Bureau, and with her husband Ernest in severely declining health and unable to work, Mary found a job cleaning floors in Keillor's jam factory. It was a short contract, which ended with a terse face off between Mary and one of the company directors. She was fired on the spot.

Her family's financial situation grew dire. Songs had sustained Mary throughout her life: songs in single end kitchen ceilidhs and in massed public acts of protest; songs as both solace and celebration; and songs in solidarity with others. With no way to make ends meet, however, Mary took to singing on the streets of Dundee. It was an economic reality that deeply shamed her dying husband but about which Mary herself was thoroughly pragmatic. Songs were a matter of survival.

Ernest died in 1943. Shortly afterwards Mary's parents came to live with her. So did her nephew Fred, for whom Mary had long played a caring role. She would look after her elderly parents for the rest of their lives. And those twenty years of day to day family care and responsibility proved also her most fertile creative period of writing.

It was following her father Sandy's death that Mary's mother Rosie encouraged her to gather her poetry and songs together. She compiled a manuscript which would eventually become *Sidlaw Breezes*. For a frustrating decade, however, she lost her only complete copy to the influential socialist songwriter and singer Ewan MacColl. She had lent it to him for his opinion and he had subsequently brought 'Oh Dear Me' into his own repertoire. It was only when MacColl finally returned her work that Mary, at the age of 69, was able to publish it. Such was her renown that the first edition sold out quickly.

It's a collection that is couthy and heartfelt, vitriolic and acerbic, naive and politically wide-ranging in its subject matter. Whilst her writing lacks the consistency or literary sophistication of MacDiarmid or Morgan, with whom she shares Parliamentary wall space, she never laid any claim to it. Her poetry is inhabited by small garden creatures and liberated by references to the restorative powers of the open Angus countryside. It is both unfettered in the spleen she directs at international warmongering and humane in its celebration of others, such as the Spanish Civil war martyr Felicia Browne. It is as erudite in its references to Hegel and Kant, Yeats and Lenin, as it is simply earthed.

Age did not diminish Mary's radicalism. In 1955, aged 58, she became chair of the Old Age Pensioners Association of Dundee. And according to Timothy Neat, in late 1970, the year I was born, Mary travelled, at the age of 73, to Hanoi in Vietnam, to tend the sick and help with the rebuilding of the ruined city. A postcard she sent to Hamish Henderson on St. Andrew's Day that year read:

> How safe I feel here. Ah Hamish how I wish we in Scotland were in this position! When I say this to the Vietnamese, they laugh – surely I must be joking! 'We are so poor' they say. If they could see us at home they would know what I mean. There is a quality of life, which seems to me, the more I know of it, like paradise – like the dreaming of all great revolutionaries.

She lived the last years of her life in a modest Dundee flat surrounded by friends and books. She died at Ninewells Hospital on March 16th 1978.

Mary is remembered now largely by the songs she left behind, several of which are still heartily sung on the Scottish folk scene. Indeed in late 1999, on my first ever recorded album, *Last Leaves* by Scots-Irish band Malinky, I sang her cheery celebration of itinerant music-making, *Love and Freedom*. In its own way the song anticipates my own transition from Children's Rights Worker to full-time writer and folk musician. Mary herself is minded in song also. Rod Paterson and the late Michael Marra, both Dundee men, dedicated their 'Bawbee Birlin' to her memory:

> O the time will come so the auld man said
> When the servant slumbers in his mester's bed If
> he's no ower busy workin overtime instead
> A for the birlin o the bawbee o't

As I see it, if a Parliament like Scotland's own is to hold a sigh within its walls, as a minding to its essential purpose, then let it be the sigh of a small woman, a working, caring, struggling, singing woman who would not keep her mouth shut, and who bore immense grief and hardship without collapsing under the weight of it.

Mary's own poem *Nae Regrets* captures her spirit best of all:

A gey rauch road, fell snell weather
A fecht tae make it a wee bit smoother
Gin we shaw our eident grit
We'll make it even better yet

Mary saw herself explicitly as a 'cheeky wee sparrow', ordinary and everyday and melodious for all that. And her writing and the arc of her life speaks to a worldly social and political vision that is rooted in a profound understanding of domesticity, toil, lifelong care for others and the intimacy of place. In my opinion, this is what women's activism and women's creativity often looks like, historically. And it helps to explain why so many of the Canongate wall inscriptions are by literary eagles and so few are by wrens.

Karine Polwart

Karine Polwart is a folk singer, songwriter and essayist. A former philosophy tutor and children's rights activist, much of her music and writing combines traditional motifs and stories with contemporary social and political observations. She is a four times winner at the BBC Radio 2 Folk Awards, including twice for Best Original Song. Her proudest musical moment was an invitation to sing at the formal opening of the 2011 session of The Scottish Parliament. She lives with her two young children in a small village in south east Scotland.

Thanks to Rebecca McKinney, Stuart Polwart and especially Liam Hurley for astute editorial feedback.

Milton Keynes UK
Ingram Content Group UK Ltd.
UKHW020626290824
447540UK00010B/139